There is something so satisf[...] slow down and create a dish[...] in the kitchen, celebrating t[...] transforming them into something magical. Murielle Banackissa—recipe developer, food stylist, and photographer—has spent hours, nights, whole weekends in her kitchen cooking for herself and for others. In *Savoring*, she shares a collection of her unique plant-based recipes that is both a celebration of those special moments found in cooking (grilling flavor into peaches to top weekend waffles, sitting with mushrooms while they caramelize) and an interweaving of her different cultural influences—from her upbringing in the Republic of Congo, to her mother's Russian and Ukrainian heritage recipes, and her family's immigration to Montreal.

With recipes that range from stuffed savory crepes to lentil-filled dumplings to cassava leaf and spinach stew, inside, you'll find:

BOUNTIFUL BREAKFASTS

Crispy Chickpea Pancakes with Avocado and Salsa; Rum-Coconut French Toast with Caramelized Bananas; Stewed Blackberries and Lemon Ricotta Toasts

SMALL PLATES AND SALADS

Pan-Fried Plantains; Pearl Barley Salad with Roasted Bell Peppers and Vegan Feta; Garlicky Miso-Glazed Bok Choy; Fufu

MARVELOUS MAIN DISHES

Coconut-Crusted Tofu with Spicy Mango Salsa; Peanut Butter and Sweet Potato Stew; Sesame Ginger Glazed Shiitakes with Sticky Rice; Quebec Meatless Pie

DELECTABLE DESSERTS

Olive Oil and Rose Polenta Bundt Cake; Spiced Poached Pear Puff Pastry Tart; Date-Sweetened Chocolate Cream Tarts; Fried Banana Beignets

With Murielle's stunning, atmospheric photography accompanying every recipe, *Savoring* is the debut cookbook from a very exciting new food talent. Filled with recipes inspired by her far-reaching family, it is a thoughtful and delicious exploration of all kinds of plant-based dishes sure to introduce new flavors to your table.

Savoring

Meaningful Vegan Recipes from Across Oceans

Murielle Banackissa

appetite
by RANDOM HOUSE

Appetite by Random House® and colophon are
registered trademarks of Penguin Random House LLC.

Library and Archives of Canada Cataloguing in
Publication is available upon request.
ISBN: 978-0-525-61179-0
eBook ISBN: 978-0-525-61180-6

Photography by Murielle Banackissa
Design by Jennifer Griffiths
Printed in China

Published in Canada by Appetite by Random House®,
a division of Penguin Random House Canada Limited

www.penguinrandomhouse.ca

10 9 8 7 6 5 4 3 2 1

appetite
by RANDOM HOUSE

PHOTOS ON THESE PAGES, LEFT TO RIGHT:
VEGGIE RICE, PAGE 130; SHUBA, PAGE 85;
BLACK BEANS AND PLANTAIN TACOS WITH
ADOBO CREMA, PAGE 179

To my mom, for always believing in me and teaching me the power of resilience, faith, and hard work.

To Sam, for seeing my passions for food and art and encouraging me to share them with the world.

Contents

DELECTABLE DESSERTS

SCRUMPTIOUS SAUCES, CREAMS, AND TOPPINGS

My Food Story and Philosophy

My earliest food memories are of my childhood in the Republic of Congo. I was born in a coastal town called Pointe-Noire, where I lived for the first eight years of my life, often heading to the beach on school lunch breaks with my mom to catch the low tide. I remember the warm, clear, light blue water, the white sand, and how far I could walk into the ocean before even half of my body was submerged in the saltwater. I was blessed to have an early childhood characterized by slow, intentional living, and a close connection to nature. I loved climbing our backyard trees to get a better view of our house, crushing tropical flowers together to create "perfume" for my mom, observing the snails and slugs that would appear on our doorstep after a torrential rainfall, and playing with colors on canvas in painting lessons. Our family had someone who cooked for us, someone who not only was a kind soul but who also made the tastiest seafood, fished directly from the Atlantic Ocean, which was mere minutes from our home. I'm talking African ghost crab, coated with a luxurious spiced and buttery glaze—it was truly finger-licking good!

Some of my most cherished memories are of the weekends after church: my family and our friends—many hailing from different continents—would gather at each other's houses with dishes of food, often from our native countries (stuffed cabbage rolls from Ukraine, sauerkraut from Estonia). Through these meals, I realized the power that food has to forge a community. All those colors, textures, and flavors were a true feast for my senses, each dish helping me develop my palate and appreciate the love and care that went into cooking it. It was the beginning of my food journey.

Of course, despite my fond memories of my early childhood in Congo, there were many reasons for my parents to start their years-long immigration process to Canada. Civil instability, recurrent power outages (sometimes lasting months), and the prevalence of diseases like malaria were all factors that pushed my parents to leave behind their jobs, friends, and a life that they knew in order to give us kids a more stable environment.

That's how, in August 2002, my family came to arrive in Montreal, Canada. There were multiple shock factors: the sounds (I never thought cities could be so loud!), the language (although Congo's main language is also French, the Quebec vocabulary and accent are unique), and, of course, the food. My mom became the primary cook in our household, which allowed her to reconnect with some of her own Russian and Ukranian culinary heritage. Although both her parents are of Russian descent, she was born in Ukraine, where she spent the first twenty-six years of her life, and is still to this day very connected to Ukrainian culture. After this cross-continental move, my mom dedicated her precious time to experimenting in the kitchen to create tasty dishes, even introducing me, my two brothers, and my father to new flavors we hadn't encountered in Congo, including foods such as broccoli, celery, blueberries, black-berries, cranberries, celeriac, and asparagus. Those first few years in Montreal brought us some of my mom's now-classic dishes—her borscht, shuba, Napoleon cake, and crepes—all of which have inspired my own food journey, as you will see in this cookbook.

My mom's now consistent presence in the kitchen inspired me to also step foot in that sacred space. Desserts especially ignited my passion to make food. In my early teenage years, I experimented with desserts by making recipes from cook-books my mom bought at thrift shops. The first recipe I attempted on my own? Crepes with chocolate sauce. I put all my heart into it. The crepes looked perfect: thin, golden, supple. They smelled heavenly too—the sweet aroma of butter and vanilla extract! But then the most unfortunate thing happened: I burned the chocolate sauce—and myself. Heartbroken and in pain, I was sure it was all ruined, that all my efforts were in vain—after all, what was the point of even serving the crepes if the chocolate sauce was inedible? But when I saw how happy my family was eating the crepes with a simple drizzle of maple syrup and some butter, and how grateful they were that I had taken the time to create something for them, I real-ized that cooking was so much more than getting a recipe perfect. It was about trial and error, taking your time, and having fun in the kitchen. It was also about pour-ing your heart into a dish that will bring

people together around the table, just like at those after-church gatherings in Congo. The chocolate-sauce incident made me realize too that I needed to sharpen my skills in the kitchen, and that would mean spending more time trying new recipes.

And that was how it started. From then on, I roamed the internet in search of the most decadent chocolate cake ever, or the most flavorful tiramisu, always trying to push myself while still impressing my family with exciting dishes. I spent my weekends in the kitchen, trying out new recipes or replicating ones my family loved. This passion for food followed me through my university years: it was always my escape, and apart from exam week, there was not one weekend that went by where I did not try out a new recipe. Cooking was a constant in my life, something I could turn to to slow down, experiment, create, and discover new flavor profiles.

Maybe because I studied international business and marketing and didn't know anyone who worked in the food industry, I had never considered pursuing a culinary career. While I dabbled in photography, it was only when it became trendy to share photos of your food on Instagram that I decided to put both my passions together. After an early opportunity to shoot for a local ice cream company, I saw my interests grow into a full-time business offering two main services: food photography and recipe development. I was just two years out of university.

Now, seven years later, my business has evolved, with recipe development becoming a core part of its architecture. I have worked with companies such as Silk, VegNews, Food52, Alter Eco, Simple Mills, and Paderno. These new opportunities also coincided with a big lifestyle change for me: becoming vegan. Being a big lover of cheese, cold meats, and seafood, I never would've thought I'd follow a fully vegan

lifestyle, but after learning about the impact of factory farming on animals and the environment, I decided to make the switch. At first, I was incredibly overwhelmed at the idea of getting all the nutrients I needed without eating any meat, fish, dairy, or eggs. I also knew very little about how to cook plant-based meals: no one close to me was vegan or even vegetarian, so I had to figure it out on my own. Like most vegans, I started by following the recipes of mainstream vegan bloggers, just to learn the basics of vegan cooking. It was a lot of fun! I dove deep into the world of spices, legumes, whole grains, sauces, and tofu, spending hours trying new recipes. I discovered dishes I had never heard of and cooking techniques that changed the way I cooked. I learned that eggs are not necessary for baking an epic chocolate cake, and that there is a wide array of plant-based alternatives to dairy products. Of course, it was not easy, and I was often tempted

to go back to animal products, but what kept me going then and continues to now is the sense of adventure I feel, and discovery of a new way to eat while finding my own voice as a recipe creator—all the while knowing that my food choices are aligned with my ethics. I am incredibly lucky that my shift to veganism happened in a time when plant-based eating was on the rise, and that many companies I worked with were looking for recipes that were more plant-forward. All of this led me to the incredible opportunity to write this, my first cookbook.

Although I had never thought I would have an opportunity of this magnitude this early on in my career, when I was approached to write a cookbook proposal, I knew almost immediately what I wanted this book to be: an ode not only to my journey but also that of my parents, who moved continents multiple times in their lives to bring me to where I am today. I wanted it to be something that represented my ancestry and my past, but also my present and my future.

Food—preparing it, sharing it—is something I want to take my time with. Through food-filled gatherings with my family's church friends in Pointe-Noire; to weekend mornings in Montreal, my mom preparing her crepes or French toasts; to my solo college weekends when I would pore over a new recipe; to meeting my husband, Sam, and discovering a whole new world of flavors through our travels together and his own family history, I've come to realize that food is an anchor, it's love. And it's my way of showing love to all those who matter to me—and now, to the world—through the recipes I share with you in this cookbook.

Dedicating an entire evening to preparing dinner, or investing a few extra moments in grilling additional flavor into the peaches to top waffles for a decadent

Sunday brunch, allows me to delve deeper into my food journey, uncovering flavors, textures, and stories behind the dishes. There is something so satisfying about choosing to consciously slow down and create a dish of my own—or to execute someone else's recipe—without distractions. I get in a zone where I am fully present and connected to the food, attentive to how it changes as it cooks slowly on the stove or bakes in the oven. And I feel a sense of excitement when a recipe calls for refrigeration to allow for the recipe to come together! Spending time in the kitchen preparing food is about love—for food, for yourself, and for others. It's about celebrating the ingredients that give us life, and dressing them up in a way that will make them stand out. Whether I am cooking for myself as an act of self-love or for others as a way to show them my love, every step of the process is permeated with this emotion.

So, this book is for the other adventurous cooks out there. The ones looking for reinvented classics and new flavors to explore. If you're looking for a book full of quick-and-easy weeknight dinners, this is not it (although a handful of the recipes might fall in that category, allowing you to still get all the flavor while on the go!). But rather, these recipes are geared toward the home cook who loves to set aside a special time on weekends or Friday night to explore new recipes, new flavors, and new cooking techniques—the cook who does not want to rush the cooking process but enjoys every step, from the browning of onions to caramelizing them to the slow stirring of the risotto and all the way to the final garnishing touch.

And, of course, this is an entirely plant-based cookbook! No recipe in it calls for any animal product, whether it be meat, fish, shellfish, eggs, or dairy. If you are already a vegan or vegetarian, great! This book will give you the perfect opportunity to expand your recipe repertoire. And good news for those who have an allergy or intolerance to nuts or seeds (I find that most trigger my eczema): while plant-based recipes elsewhere often rely on nuts and seeds as a prominent ingredient, you will be able to make nearly all the recipes here with no modification (read more about this on page 8)! If you are not vegan or vegetarian but want to explore that world without sacrificing flavor, I have a feeling you'll have fun with this cookbook. With this book, I want to redefine what it means to be vegan today by bringing more soul, depth, culture, and flavor to the vegan scene.

When it comes to my food philosophy, I place the most importance on flavor. I love food that is very well seasoned and well rounded. However, every person's palate is different, so I truly encourage you to take control of the seasoning as you make the recipes in this book. Take the time to find what's right for you; don't be afraid to adjust ingredients and seasonings to your liking, and to explore to find the techniques and ingredients that speak to your soul. Do not rush through the process; instead, slow down to allow the flavors to slowly unravel as you walk through each recipe step. I also very much value health. I love developing recipes that are both nourishing and flavorful. Through the years, I have come to realize that finding what is right for each of us is key to fostering an enjoyable relationship with our food.

I am super excited that you will be diving into this cookbook and exploring my corner of the culinary universe. Pour yourself a glass of wine, kombucha, or iced lemon water, and comb through these pages to discover my recipes.

Notes on the Recipes

I love to make cooking an intentional activity, one in which I am fully present with the food, allowing myself time to experiment and for flavors to bloom. I want to share some of the philosophies I bring with me each time I step foot in the kitchen, detailing how they translate into the time I spend in that sacred space. Of course, like any philosophy, you must choose what feels true and right to you and what does not. As you spend more time in the kitchen, I encourage you to discover your own cooking philosophies.

TASTE-AND-ADJUST

This is a philosophy I hold dear to my heart. One of the things I love most about cooking is the process of discovery and finding what flavors resonate the most. Everyone has a different palate, therefore who am I to say that ¼ teaspoon of salt is the *perfect* amount of seasoning? I for one always modify others' recipes to my liking, especially when it comes to those savory dishes in which the flavors develop as you cook them (as opposed to cakes, say, where the flavor is developed as they bake in the oven). Tasting and adjusting is key to creating a recipe that reflects your preferences. So what does this look like when cooking? Let's say you are making

my Ultimate Breakfast Sandwich (p. 57). The recipe calls for 2 tablespoons of vegan mayo mixed with 2 teaspoons of sambal oelek or sriracha, but you are really sensitive to heat. Just start off with ½ teaspoon of the hot sauce and build your way up. I view most recipes as starting points, and although every recipe in this book is tasty as written, each also reflects my own preferences. Chances are yours will be different. So every time you find yourself in the kitchen cooking, be sure to taste and adjust.

LETTING TIME DO ITS MAGIC

I know that oftentimes when we cook, we're in a rush. We are hungry or want to get our meal ready quickly. It's frequently the case with me. However, in those times when I don't rush through the cooking process, I know I end up with a much better result than I would otherwise have. When I actually let the onions cook down and slightly caramelize, as opposed to cooking them only until they're barely translucent, the flavors of my dish are dramatically altered. Throughout the recipe instructions, I offer time cues for cooking that I hope will help you assess just how long to cook certain ingredients. Of course, these are just indicators and can vary depending on the type and size of pan you use or the power of your stove, but they are there as guidelines to remind you to let time (and heat) do its magic. Flavors bloom with time, and while super-quick recipes have their place, some moments are meant for slowing down.

REPLACING/SWAPPING INGREDIENTS

Growing up, I used to be *so* strict when it came to following a recipe. Whenever I found myself in the kitchen with my mom, who is the ultimate improviser, I would always be so annoyed when she swapped out even two ingredients in a recipe! I mean, how can you make a spaghetti sauce that calls for celery when you don't have celery?! After spending countless hours in the kitchen myself, taking chances and realizing that what makes cooking an art form is the playing around with ingredients, adapting recipes to what's in your pantry and letting your preferences influence the recipes, I became a lot more flexible in my cooking. Of course, I would never suggest making a risotto with quinoa instead of arborio rice, but I would say that if you don't have vegetable broth but do have vegan chicken broth on hand, that is perfectly okay to use. If you don't have vegan butter but do have vegan margarine, use that. Sure, the end result might be a little different from what the recipe author created in *their* kitchen, but that is the magic of cooking! After all, two people can make the same recipe, using the *same* ingredients, and yet the results might be quite different. Of course, not everyone necessarily knows which ingredients are good substitutes for others, so I've included a "customizable" icon at those recipes where you can play around with the ingredient list a little more and still obtain equally delicious results—simply watch for the details on which ingredients can be swapped.

ICONS

CUSTOMIZABLE: As discussed, this icon indicates whether a recipe's ingredient list has a fair bit of flexibility—for example, if a vegetable or an herb can be swapped for another. Recipes with this icon are a great place to start exploring flavors and adapting dishes based on what you have on hand and your preferences.

GLUTEN-FREE: This icon identifies any recipe that is either already gluten-free or has an option to easily be made so.

NUT/SEED-FREE: This icon identifies any recipe that is either already entirely nut- or seed-free or has an option to easily be made so. This includes peanuts—even though they are a legume—to make it easy for those who have this common allergy.

EXTRA PREP/TIME: This icon indicates any recipe that requires a more than average amount of preparation and/or a longer than average amount of time. This might mean that an extended amount of resting time is involved in the recipe, or that preparing another recipe in this cookbook is necessary first—for example, in order to make my Ricotta and Spinach Phyllo Cups (p. 111), you need to make the Nut-Free Ricotta (p. 264) first—or that a recipe takes more than 1½ hours in total to complete. I've added this icon to help you better plan your time in the kitchen.

MIXING BOWL SIZES

Have you ever been mixing ingredients in a bowl, only to have some spill over the sides, making a huge mess and instantly regreting not opting to use a bigger bowl? I am definitely raising both hands for that one! So my philosophy now is *Aim bigger!* I have a set of variously sized stainless steel mixing bowls, and I absolutely *love them.* The ones I use the most often in my day-to-day cooking are (you guessed it) the two largest! If you have experienced bowl spillage in the past, I highly recommend investing in a set so that you have options of sizes to choose from, so you can stir and mix without spillage.

PAN SIZES

Throughout this book, I share the sizes of baking pans I use for cakes, bars, rolls, and tarts along with the baking time required for those recipes. However, I know that not everyone necessarily has those sizes of pans, but as long as you have the right shape of pan in a fairly similar size, don't worry about it—you can still make the recipe! All you have to keep in mind is that the pan size will affect the baking time. My tip: If using a pan smaller than the suggested size, check the dish every 5 minutes or so once it's beyond the suggested baking time, paying close attention to readiness cues (for example, a toothpick inserted into the center comes out clean). On the other hand, if your pan is bigger than the suggested size, remove 10 minutes from the baking time, check for readiness once your timer goes off, and continue baking if necessary until the dish is ready.

WEIGHING INGREDIENTS

Up until a few months before writing this cookbook, the vast majority of recipes I created were measured in cups and spoons only. However, something I realized while observing how other people cook is that the way ingredients are measured can vary greatly from person to person (see below for an example with flour). Because of this, I've also provided the metric weights for ingredients of 1 tablespoon or more for all the baking recipes, and for any other recipe where the precise measurement of ingredients could make a noticeable difference to its success. Of course, these weights are just there to guide you; if you feel confident about properly measuring

flour (using the *fluff, scoop, fill, shave* method described below) and other ingredients, simply use the cup and spoon measurements.

HOW TO MEASURE FLOUR CORRECTLY: For any of this book's recipes that involve flour, whether they be for bread, cakes, pancakes, or waffles, I used one measuring technique when it comes to cup measures: fluff, scoop, fill, shave. This involves fluffing up the flour in the flour bag or jar with a spoon, scooping it out to fill the measuring cup, and then shaving off the little mountain of flour on top with the flat side of a butter knife. This technique, as opposed to my husband's way of directly scooping out the flour from the bag with a measuring cup and shaking it to obtain an evenly filled (and packed!) cup, ensures that you are not measuring too much flour and results in lighter baked goods. And, as I mentioned, recipes for baked goods in the breakfast and dessert chapters also give the flour measurement in metric weight, so that you can measure it more precisely.

SAUTÉING MUSHROOMS

I had to really hold myself back from creating tons of mushroom recipes for this book, as mushrooms are one of my favorite ingredients to cook with. When it comes to sautéing mushrooms, what's most important is the size of the pan. Always use one big enough to allow the mushrooms to lie flat in a single (or almost single) layer. Also be sure to use medium-high or high heat when sautéing them. Doing this will ensure that your mushrooms come out beautifully caramelized. Last but not least, let time and heat do its magic. Do not try to rush the caramelization; instead, enjoy the process of seeing your food transform before your eyes. Wait until their edges turn a beautiful golden brown before salting them—salting releases moisture, which can stall the caramelization.

Notes on Ingredients

Here's a list of pretty much all the staples I have in my kitchen. Keep in mind that I photograph food and develop recipes for a living, so the list is fairly exhaustive. In many cases, swaps are totally possible, as you'll see from the options below. By spending more time in the kitchen and developing your own cooking style and preferences, you will come to discover which pantry staples are a must for you.

BAKING ESSENTIALS

BAKING POWDER AND BAKING SODA: Both of these powders are used as leavening agents to help baked goods rise.

CHOCOLATE: I always have two kinds of chocolate on hand: chips (mini and regular-sized) and bars. I use bittersweet (50 to 70%) vegan chocolate chips mostly for cookies and for The Chocolate Microwave Cake of Your Dreams (p. 235), to add sweetness and decadence to the batter. For the rest of my recipes, including The Best Chocolate Frosting (p. 272) and Chocolate Kolbasa (p. 211), I chop up 85% dark chocolate bars; this balances out the other very sweet ingredients (like dates and store-bought cookies). If you have a real sweet tooth, a good place to start in the dark-chocolate department is with 70% chocolate. I try my best to buy fair-trade chocolate whenever I can, to support fairer treatment of small-scale cacao growers.

COCOA POWDER: Rich and slightly bitter, cocoa powder is a must for many chocolatey desserts. The kind I use most often is organic Dutch-processed.

COCONUT WHIPPING CREAM: Whipped cream is a food you can still enjoy when you're a vegan—by using coconut whipping cream. I know, however, that the struggle can be real when it comes to finding the brand that makes the best coconut whipping cream. Here are my favorites:

○ Cha's Organics makes my absolute favorite coconut whipping cream. You can buy it on well.ca. This is a heavy whipping cream that comes out of the can thick and creamy: no liquid separates during refrigeration. The entire can can be used to make the fluffiest whipping cream that holds together wonderfully well!

○ Silk has a coconut whipping cream in a carton, similar to the traditional dairy kind. If you're whipping this up, make sure to use about a third less than the recipe calls for, as it expands way more than cream from a can.

∘ Savoy coconut cream is another good alternative. It's sold in a can and needs to be refrigerated for at least 8 hours before scooping out the cream that separated itself from the water. It also whips up beautifully and holds together well.

∘ Native Forest classic coconut milk is also a good option. After refrigerating the can, you will be able to scoop out the cream at the top and whip it up. But because this is milk rather than cream, you'll get less cream than you would from the other suggestions above.

CORNSTARCH: Cornstarch is my go-to thickening agent. Some people hesitate to use it because some corn crops are GMO (though buying organic solves that problem), but I've found that alternatives don't thicken liquids as much as cornstarch does and can even make the liquids feel slimy. However, if texture is not that big of an issue for you or if you're trying to avoid corn products, feel free to switch out the cornstarch in my recipes with another thickener of choice, like arrowroot or tapioca powder.

EGG REPLACER: Some of the recipes in this book use egg replacers, none of which is a premade product (like vegan liquid egg or powdered egg, which can be difficult to track down). The ones I call for most often are either flax or chia eggs (ground flax or chia seeds mixed with water) and unsweetened applesauce. In many of my baked goods, you might not even see an obvious egg replacer in the ingredient list, but know that I've chosen and measured all the ingredients carefully to ensure that the recipe works

without one—yes, vegan cakes can be moist and tasty even without eggs and egg replacers!

FLAVOR EXTRACTS: The extract most commonly used in my recipes is vanilla extract. It's a subtle extract that adds a slightly sweet and aromatic flavor to any dessert. I also like having a few floral extracts in my pantry, such as orange blossom and rosewater, which is featured in My Olive Oil and Rose Polenta Bundt Cake (p. 245).

FLOURS

ALL-PURPOSE FLOUR: I know all-purpose flour has gotten a lot of negative press over the past few years, especially in the vegan community, since it is made of refined wheat. Although I absolutely love alternative flours and cook or bake with them all the time, all-purpose flour will *always* have a place in my pantry. I love to use it particularly for baking because it adds lightness to baked goods, like my Piña Colada Cakes (p. 209) and my Fried Banana Beignets (p. 223). If you are gluten-free, Bob's Red Mill Gluten-Free 1-to-1 Baking Flour is a great alternative.

CHICKPEA FLOUR: If you had asked me before I went vegan whether it's possible to create flour out of legumes, I would have said, "Yeah, sure, but are these flours any good in the kitchen?" Lo and behold, the answer is *yes*! Chickpea flour is one of those legume flours that has become a staple in my pantry. As the name implies, it's made of ground chickpeas. It can be used in both savory and sweet recipes, but I love to use it most to make my family-famous Crispy Chickpea Pancakes (p. 41) and The Only Chocolate Chip Cookies I Will Ever Make (p. 241).

TIGERNUT FLOUR: When I realized I am intolerant of most nuts, almost all desserts that called for nut or seed flours became inaccessible to me. Until I found tigernut flour, that is. Made of ground tigernuts—which are actually tubers (like potatoes), not nuts—tigernut flour has a wonderful nutty flavor and helps give baked goods an extra chewy texture. I have found it to be a great nut-free substitute for most nut or seed flours, including the very popular almond flour.

WHOLE-SPELT FLOUR: I have found that whole spelt is an excellent alternative to whole-wheat flour. So, if my recipe calls for whole-wheat flour and you don't have any, but you do have whole-spelt flour on hand, feel free to substitute it. Like whole-wheat flour, whole-spelt flour is hearty and satisfying thanks to its high amount of protein and fiber. It also has gluten, which means that by using it in baked goods, you will not compromise on the stretchiness and doughy-ness wheat flour provides.

WHOLE-WHEAT FLOUR: If I had to choose only one flour to have in my pantry for the rest of my life, it would be whole-wheat flour. It is inexpensive, is super easy to find, has extra fiber and protein to keep me full longer, and works in a variety of recipes.

FRUITS AND VEGETABLES

It's not possible to list every single fruit and veggie I consume or feature in this book! In general, I gravitate toward local produce when it is in season, for multiple reasons. First, it is generally cheaper when it's in season than when it is not. Second, it tends to taste better. Of course, in Canada, where I live, there isn't a whole lot of produce that grows year-round (although now there is more locally grown greenhouse produce, which has been great!), so when I crave certain fruits or vegetables that are not in season here in the wintertime, I buy fresh produce from the US or Mexico, or turn to frozen products to keep my menu options open. Whenever I call for fruits or vegetables in my recipes, I'll note whether they are swappable and with what. If you can use a frozen alternative, I'll mention that too.

GRAINS AND PASTA

ARBORIO RICE: Also known as *the risotto rice*, arborio rice can absorb lots of liquid, and becomes creamy and slightly chewy when cooked. Apart from using it in risotto, I always have arborio rice on hand just in case I have a craving for my childhood's Creamy Coconut Rice Pudding (p. 54).

BROWN BASMATI RICE: Similar to white basmati rice in shape but higher in fiber and protein, brown basmati rice is a rice I love for its chewy texture and subtle nutty flavor. Like most grains, it works well as a side, but I also incorporate it in recipes, particularly in my Veggie Rice (p. 130).

PASTA: I *love* carbs, and pasta is no exception. At any time, you can find a wide array of pasta in my pantry. From whole-wheat to white, gluten-free to legume-based, pasta works great as a base for a dish and is honestly wonderful as a snack—I mean, is there anything better than a bit of orzo cooked to perfection and drizzled with extra virgin olive oil?

PEARL BARLEY: The first time I ate pearl barley was in Salzburg, Austria. Our couch-surfing host made it for Sam and me, and I remember being mind-blown by its chewy texture and soft exterior. Although it is delicious as a side of its own, I love it most incorporated in salads, in particular in my Pearl Barley Salad with Roasted Bell Peppers and Vegan Feta (p. 113).

QUINOA: A small round grain that is a little nutty and earthy in flavor, quinoa is one of my go-to grains as a side. Ready in under 30 minutes, and protein- and fiber-packed, it fills me up for a while and pairs well with most other side dishes. Some people find that rinsing it takes away a little of its bitterness, but I don't rinse mine anymore and I haven't noticed a big difference.

WHITE BASMATI RICE: For me, white rice is the grain I make when I want to feel like I'm at a restaurant. Since at home Sam and I prefer opting for grains that are a little more filling, and more protein- and fiber-packed most weekdays, white rice rarely makes it onto our plates. *However,* when we make an elaborate dish like Saka Saka (p. 133), we just *love* accompanying it with white rice. And it is the perfect grain for Coconut Rice (p. 100)—my favorite!

NONDAIRY MILKS

COCONUT MILK: Two kinds of coconut milk I use in the recipes in this book are unsweetened coconut beverage and full-fat coconut milk from a can. Coconut beverage is usually sold in a carton and while, like coconut milk, its base is coconut cream and water, it's also often fortified with vitamins. It's considerably lighter in texture and fat content than full-fat coconut milk and therefore, in my opinion, works better in baked goods where I want to infuse a coconut flavor without weighing them down. Canned coconut milk is a lot richer and fattier than coconut beverage and is used to add creaminess to sweet and savory dishes. When choosing canned coconut milk, I always look for one that contains only two ingredients: coconut and water—no stabilizers.

UNSWEETENED SOY MILK: Unsweetened soy milk is my absolute go-to for all the recipes that require a nondairy milk other than full-fat coconut milk. Because I am intolerant to most nuts *and* oats, I stay away from other kinds of nondairy milks. Not only do I *love* the flavor of soy, but it is affordable and packed with protein. I simply make sure to buy organic soy milk, which doesn't contain GMOs. Throughout this book, whenever you encounter unsweetened soy milk in a recipe, you can replace it with your favorite unsweetened nondairy milk in a carton—except for in my Nut-Free Ricotta (p. 264), which requires the high protein content of soy milk in order to curdle properly.

NUTS AND SEEDS

As I've mentioned, I'm rather sensitive to most nuts and seeds. Although I will indulge from time to time in a cashew-based cheesecake or cheese, or in a sunflower seed–loaded veggie pâté, my intolerance to nuts and seeds makes it so that I seldom buy, cook, and bake with them (unless it's for work). Listed below are the six nuts and seeds I am least sensitive to and therefore are used in my recipes. I've also noted in a few recipes where you can add nuts, if you don't have an allergy or sensitivity to them, such as my Chocolate Cardamom Oat-Free Granola (p. 53) and Massaged Kale Salad (p. 97).

CHIA AND FLAX SEEDS: I tend to buy chia and flax seeds whole and then grind them in batches as needed, to better absorb their nutrients. They're often cheaper purchased this way and will stay fresh longer. I use chia and flax seeds mixed with a bit of water for egg replacers when baking. I also use them in smoothies to add extra protein, fiber, and omega-3s.

HEMP HEARTS: If I had to choose my favorite seed, I would say it's hemp hearts. Their subtle taste is reminiscent of both sunflower seeds and pine nuts. Add hemp hearts to smoothies, sprinkle them on a toast with peanut butter and homemade jam, or into salads. Tip: Costco may beat other stores on price!

PEANUTS: What would I do without peanuts? This legume has been my saving grace ever since I linked my eczema to my nuts and seeds consumption. Although I love peanut butter in desserts, in this cookbook you will see peanuts more frequently in savory dishes. Since peanut allergies are so common, this book's recipes that contain peanuts are not considered nut-free—even if they don't contain other nuts.

PISTACHIOS AND HAZELNUTS: What are the odds that of all nuts out there, the two I react to the least are two of the most expensive?! Oh well, sometimes Mother Nature is totally unpredictable. At least I absolutely love both of these nuts and think they work super well in a variety of dishes, both sweet and savory. Hence, you will find that they're often sprinkled onto my dishes. Of course, since I highly encourage you to adapt my recipes to your wants, needs, preferences, budget, and whatever ingredients you have on hand, if you aren't allergic to other nuts or seeds and feel they'd better suit you, feel free to use them instead. In the recipes calling for pistachios or hazelnuts, I specify which other nut or seed (if any) would work best as a replacement.

SESAME SEEDS: I rarely consume sesame seeds on their own. However, I have them somewhat often in the form of tahini, which is a rich paste made of ground sesame seeds. Tahini is terrific as a base for a creamy salad dressing, added to smoothies, or in a rich noodle sauce when paired with tamari, sriracha, rice vinegar, and maple syrup. You can also use it instead of your favorite nut butter in my recipe for The Only Chocolate Chip Cookies I Will Ever Make (p. 241).

OILS AND BUTTERS

AVOCADO OIL: Avocado oil is my go-to oil for so many reasons. It has a neutral taste, so it can work in virtually any dish. It also has a high smoke point, meaning I can use it in most of my cooking, including for frying food—though I only use it for shallow frying because it is relatively expensive (that said, I've found that buying this oil at Costco is a good option, as the package size is much bigger than that found at other stores and the price per milliliter is lower). This is the oil used most often in the recipes in this cookbook.

CANOLA OIL: I always have a bottle of canola oil on hand in my kitchen in case I get an unstoppable desire to fry up some vegan goodies. This oil, like avocado oil, has a high smoke point and is neutral in flavor, which makes it versatile and suitable for most tasks in the kitchen. It is also the one that I prefer when making Congolese-inspired dishes, as the flavor really brings me back to my childhood. Plus, of all the oils on this list, it is the cheapest per milliliter.

COCONUT OIL: Both refined and virgin coconut oils can be used to replace vegan butter. I like to have both on hand for different purposes. The refined kind (also known as deodorized coconut oil) is the one I use mostly for homemade vegan cheeses, to ensure they have no coconut flavor whatsoever. It can also be used to grease pans when baking or as a neutral cooking oil. As for the virgin kind, I use this when I want to infuse a little bit of coconut flavor into what I am making, or for a coconut-forward dessert when I want the coconut flavor to be *everywhere*, like in my Piña Colada Cakes (p. 209). Don't worry, the recipes will specify which kind of coconut oil to use.

COOKING SPRAY: Fun fact: greasing pans is one of the things I *really* dislike in baking! When I baked cakes when I was young, I always hoped that my mom would volunteer to grease the cake pans. Back then, we used the inside of the wrapping paper from a block of butter to grease the pans, and I found the whole process messy and, frankly, not very fun. Then we discovered cooking spray. I was instantly converted. At Costco (I am in no way affiliated with Costco—I am just a fan!), we'd get these massive cans of cooking spray that would last for ages—about two years—and made greasing any pan a walk in the park. But since not everyone uses cooking spray, in the recipes where I suggest using it, I also offer an alternative (such as melted vegan butter, coconut oil, or another liquid oil that complements the dish).

OLIVE OIL: A good-quality extra virgin olive oil can really bring out the flavors of a dish—and add a whole new depth of flavor. I use olive oil when I want the flavor of the oil to be discernable, like in salads as well as in dishes such as my Crispy Chickpea Pancakes with Avocado and Salsa (p. 41) and Roasted Cauliflower with Caper-Raisin Sauce (p. 109).

TOASTED SESAME OIL: Sesame oil is not an oil I use for cooking but rather as a flavor booster in sauces. This oil is very aromatic with its rich notes of toasted sesame. I use it to add a touch of smokiness to my dishes, and it works wonderfully in many Asian-inspired dishes. This oil is a pantry must because it can really take a dish to another level in terms of flavor.

VEGAN BUTTER (UNSALTED AND SALTED): When I first became vegan, there were very few vegan butter options on the market, and pretty much all of them were expensive. With the passing of time and the rise of veganism, many affordable options are now available, which is why I have started incorporating vegan butter into my baking. Vegan butter can add a traditional butter aroma to baked goods, so I always have it on hand. Recipes in this book use unsalted vegan butter. If you have only salted butter on hand, just reduce or leave out the salt called for in the recipe. If you do not have vegan butter, vegan margarine works as a replacement in most cases, except for in recipes that require the butter to be hard (scones, pie crusts). In those cases, use hard coconut oil (either refined or virgin). If using vegan margarine, which is salted, make sure to reduce or eliminate the salt in the recipe.

PLANT-BASED CHEESES

Since I can consume small quantities of cashews without too much consequence, and because many cashew cheeses, which tend to be fermented, often have more pronounced flavors than other types of nut-free cheeses, I do have them in my pantry from time to time (especially during the holiday season!). Most frequently, though, I opt for nut-free cheeses from brands such as Violife and Nafsika's Garden. I use plant-based cheese in the same way as dairy cheese: in gourmet grilled cheeses, sprinkling it on spaghetti, and adding it to quesadillas and tacos.

PROTEIN

BEANS: Beans are a staple in my pantry. Not only do they provide protein and sustenance, they also work well in a variety of recipes. I buy them both dried and canned. My favorites are black, white navy, mung, and pinto.

Dried beans cost less than canned beans, but you have to cook them before using. For years, I would simply soak the beans, then cook them on the stovetop for 1 to 2 hours, until fork-tender. Since receiving a pressure cooker as a gift, though, I've been cooking my beans in it. For finding out how long to cook each type of bean in a pressure cooker, the internet is your friend.

I like to have canned beans in my pantry for those times when I start making a recipe calling for beans, only to realize that I have no precooked beans on hand.

LEGUMES: Apart from the beans mentioned above, I cook a lot with lentils (brown and red) as well as with chickpeas. Brown lentils add texture to chunky sauces and salads, as they hold together quite well, whereas red lentils soften considerably when cooked, making them perfect for creamy stews and blending into soups. Chickpeas, on the other hand, have a hearty texture. My favorite way to use them is in homemade hummus, but also in stews and mashed up alongside other ingredients in a sandwich.

TOFU: I am a tofu *lover* now. *Truly.* Before going vegan, I never understood how people could eat and actually enjoy tofu. It always seemed like such a bland ingredient to me. But you know what? *That* is where its beauty lies. Because it is neutral in flavor, it works beautifully in so many recipes! From savory dishes to sweet dishes and even smoothies, tofu is an absolute all-star in the kitchen. The key is knowing how to prepare it. In this book, recipes may call for one of two types of tofu: extra-firm for savory dishes, and silken tofu for sweet dishes.

TVP: Textured vegetable protein is made of soy flour. It is very high in protein and fiber and is a good substitute for meat in vegan recipes. Although it is not my go-to ingredient when cooking, it's one worth having on hand for when you want to bulk up a saucy dish, such as spaghetti sauce. In this book you will find this ingredient in my TVP Rice and Beans (p. 198), an adaptation on one of my mom's classic dishes.

SEASONINGS

HERBS AND SPICES: Herbs and spices are the ultimate flavor boosters in a dish. I rely mostly on dried herbs and spices in my cooking, but I love fresh herbs such as dill, parsley, green onions, chives, and coriander to add a bit of greenery to a dish and an extra pop of flavor. Some of my go-to dried herbs and spices are oregano, thyme, cardamom (ground or whole), cayenne pepper, chili powder, Chinese five spice, cinnamon (ground), coriander (ground or seeds), cumin (ground or seeds), mild curry powder, garlic powder, ginger (ground), nutmeg (whole), onion powder, paprika (sweet or smoked), and turmeric (ground).

HOT SAUCE (SAMBAL OELEK AND SRIRACHA): There was a time in my life when I was obsessed with hot sauce; sriracha would make its way into literally every single savory dish I would eat in a day. Times have changed. Now I use hot sauces sporadically and mostly for flavor and a little kick, as opposed to using them for actual *heat.* The hot sauces I cook with

most often are sambal oelek (similar in taste to sriracha, but less sweet, chunkier, and a little spicier), which I love mostly for dips or folded into my Crispy Chickpea Pancakes with Avocado and Salsa (p. 41), and sriracha (I love its smooth texture and it can be more easily found in large grocery chains). These sauces can be used interchangeably in the recipes in this book.

LEMON AND LIME: Have you ever added a squeeze of lemon or lime juice to a dish and suddenly found yourself in front of what suddenly seemed like a completely different dish? Acidity has the power to balance out flavors, waking up the subtleties of other ingredients, and sometimes taming heat or salt levels. Because I am not a big vinegar person, I often rely on lemon and lime to add brightness to my salad dressings.

NUTRITIONAL YEAST: Before going vegan, I thought a cheesy flavor could come only from actual cheese. Little did I know there existed a yellow, flaky ingredient that could add cheesiness to any dish, without any dairy. Apart from its cheesy flavor, nutritional yeast is also savory and has notes of umami, making it a great ingredient to add to countless recipes and one I *always* have on hand.

SALT AND PEPPER: The simplest place to start when it comes to seasonings is with salt and pepper. I use sea salt for all my cooking (and, occasionally, black salt or kala namak) but do like to use coarser salt as garnish. My two favorites are fleur de sel and simple coarse sea salt. When it comes to pepper, if you have not converted to using freshly cracked pepper, you must! Preground pepper simply does not compare with freshly cracked pepper in terms of flavor and kick. I use a mortar and pestle

to grind small batches of whole black pepper, but you could also use a pepper or spice grinder.

TAMARI OR SOY SAUCE: Tamari is a holy grail item in my kitchen. When I go out of town and know I will be cooking, I *always* bring a bottle of this liquid goodness with me to season and add depth of flavor to virtually anything. Tamari is savory, like soy sauce, but it also has sweet, umami, and almost meaty notes. Most often, I choose tamari over soy sauce, because I find the flavor to be more complex and less salty. I always buy it in bulk at Costco, where the price is the same as at grocery stores but for more than double the quantity! If tamari is not available to you for whatever reason, just use soy sauce. However, I suggest opting for a reduced-sodium soy sauce and tasting your dish as you go to ensure that the salt levels are to your liking.

SWEETENERS

DATES: Incredibly sweet and chewy, dates are a fabulous way to naturally sweeten dishes. There are more than a dozen varieties of dates, but my go-tos are Bam (also known as Mazafati), Habibi, Medjool, and Noor. Most recipes in this book featuring dates can be made using any variety, including the rather dry ones (Deglet Noor), which you simply need to soak in hot water before using. My Date-Sweetened Leek and Onion Jam (p. 270), however, requires soft dates.

MAPLE SYRUP: If you could measure a person's Canadian-ness by their love of maple syrup, I would be a true Canadian. I love anything maple-flavored, and whenever I can use maple syrup as a sweetener, I do. It has notes of caramel and adds richness to desserts. It is also a good sweetener for savory dishes, since, as a liquid sweetener, it does not need to dissolve to be easily incorporated. I tend to opt for dark maple syrup because of its more pronounced maple flavor.

ORGANIC CANE SUGAR, BROWN SUGAR, AND POWDERED SUGAR:

In the recipes in this book, I use all three of these sugars. Instead of standard granulated sugar, I opt for organic cane sugar, but if you only have the former on hand, it does work as a one-to-one substitute. As for brown sugar, I use organic light or dark brown sugar interchangeably. And I always have powdered sugar on hand because it makes for such a simple yet beautiful garnish on many desserts or sweet brunch dishes. Just as with chocolate, I try to opt for brands that follow fair trade practices.

VEGETABLE BROTH

My go-to vegetable broth is the concentrate from Better Than Bouillon. I simply dilute 1 teaspoon of it in 1 cup of boiling water. Whenever I want to infuse a chicken or beef flavor into a vegan dish, I opt for vegan/plant-based chicken- or beef-flavored vegan stock cubes by double checking that the ingredient list does not contain animal products. Better Than Bouillon also offers vegan "No Chicken" and "No Beef" bases.

VINEGARS

I am absolutely *not* a vinegar nerd! I know many food bloggers who have a slew of vinegars for various recipes and uses, but I rely on only four. These four have fulfilled all my acidic needs and desires in the kitchen!

APPLE CIDER VINEGAR: Apple cider vinegar has subtle notes of apple and honey and therefore is suited to salad dressings, but I most often use it in baking, as it activates baking soda, allowing my cakes to rise high and to be light and airy.

BALSAMIC VINEGAR: Complex in flavor, rich, and slightly sweet, balsamic vinegar is a true staple in my kitchen. If you can afford to buy one that is aged, I encourage you to: you will be super impressed with the depth of flavor it can add to a dish. I most often use balsamic vinegar in dressings, including in my Tamari, Balsamic Vinegar, and Nutritional Yeast Sauce (p. 261), but I also like to reduce it on the stovetop until it is nice and thick, then drizzle it over salads or pizzas as a sweet finishing touch.

RICE VINEGAR: Nine times out of ten when I use tamari or soy sauce, I balance the saltiness with a touch of acidity, and one of my go-tos for doing that is unseasoned rice vinegar. This vinegar is slightly sour and sweet, and not too astringent, making it a tasty addition to sautéed mushrooms, grilled bok choy, peanut butter dips for Vietnamese rolls, salad dressings, and so much more.

WHITE VINEGAR: In the kitchen, I use white vinegar for only one thing: pickled veggies. Ever since I discovered how easy it is to make my own pickled red onion, it has been a staple in my fridge, and the key ingredient for it is white vinegar. You can find the recipe for my ultra-customizable pickled onions on page 267.

Notes on Equipment

Kitchen tools help prepping, cooking, and baking processes run smoothly. In this section, I share with you the tools I use on the daily, and ones I use less regularly but still have in my arsenal.

3-IN-1 HAND BLENDER: This is a kitchen tool that comes with a hand-held blender with changeable attachments: immersion blender, whisk, and mini food processor. I have been in love with this tool ever since my mom got hers years ago and I witnessed how useful it is. The immersion blender attachment is handy for pureeing sauces or soups without transferring them to a high-speed blender. Of course, even if you own the most powerful 3-in-1 hand blender, chances are it might not result in the smoothest sauces or soups, but in my experience it does a really great job! Also, the whisk attachment is useful if you do not own a hand or stand mixer. I use mine to whip up my coconut whipped cream and sometimes to whisk cake batter. Last but not least, the mini food processor is handy for chopping small quantities of veggies or fruits, and for small batches of pesto or jam. If you are looking to purchase one of these, consider opting for one with variable speeds, for the most flexibility.

BAKING DISHES: I recommend having these baking dishes in your kitchen:

○ A standard baking sheet (13 × 18 inches), for roasting veggies and for baking pizzas and flatbreads.

○ A square baking dish (9 × 9 inches or 8 × 8 inches), for brownies, bars, and squares.

BAMBOO CUTTING BOARD: I dislike cutting on glass cutting boards, as I find them to be a little loud. Although plastic boards are an option, they scratch easily and stain quickly. Therefore, my go-to material for a cutting board is bamboo. It is durable, not loud, low maintenance, hygienic, and does not scratch.

CHEF'S KNIFE: I know there are people who love small knives and use them all the time. However, I am not one of them. My go-to knife is a large 10-inch chef's knife. I use it for all my food cutting. One thing that is important, though: *sharpen your knife!* I cannot begin to tell you how big of a difference it will make to your cooking experience. As I can attest to, few things are as frustrating as trying to slice a bell pepper with a dull knife!

DIGITAL KITCHEN SCALE: It is only in recent years that I started using a kitchen scale. As I mentioned in the section on weighing ingredients (p. 9), I find it particularly useful when baking to ensure that measurements are accurate so that my baked goods come out perfect every time. I also use it for recipes that call for ingredients that are a little hard to measure—for example, my Watermelon "Tuna" recipe (p. 89), where how much watermelon is in 1 cup depends on how closely you follow the cutting instructions. Therefore, in these types of instances, a scale will help the measurement be as accurate as possible.

DUTCH OVEN (OR ANY OTHER LARGE HEAVY-BOTTOMED POT): I think a large heavy-bottomed pot is essential in every kitchen. Although I love a Dutch oven for its versatility (I bake bread in it as well as cook one-pot dishes), any large, solid pot will be useful for the recipes in this book, including for my Veggie Rice (p. 130), Saka Saka (p. 133), and Peanut Butter and Sweet Potato Stew (p. 141).

FOOD PROCESSOR: My food processor is not a fancy model but actually one of the cheapest on the market. It is one of the most useful kitchen tools! For chopping or grating large amounts of veggies, making homemade pesto and creamy spreads, and even breaking down vegan butter and pulsing it with flour to create a flaky pie crust, this tool is incredibly versatile.

STAINLESS STEEL OR GLASS MIXING BOWLS: Mixing bowls are a must in my kitchen. Treat yourself to a full set of sizes, and remember, always aim bigger (see page 8).

GRILL CAST-IRON PAN: Given that I do not own a barbecue, I use a grill cast-iron pan to grill virtually every vegetable, be it corn, bell peppers, shishito peppers, onions, zucchini, cherry tomatoes, mushrooms, and more. It can also be used to make restaurant-style sandwiches and grilled cheeses, as well as for grilling tofu and infusing it with a little smoky flavor, like in my Peanut Butter and Sweet Potato Stew (p. 141).

HIGH-SPEED BLENDER: I have had my high-speed blender (a Vitamix) for more than ten years now and, I have to say, it has been absolutely worth the investment. Yes, it was expensive, but it comes in handy almost daily for me. For everything from blending large quantities of sauces—like for my Smoky Sweet Potato Mac and Cheese (p. 135)—to making silky smooth smoothies, banana ice cream, homemade nut butters, or plant-based milks, a high-speed blender is a tool that has become essential in my kitchen.

MEASURING CUPS AND SPOONS: I think it goes without saying that I use these every time I follow a recipe or test one of my own. They are probably the most common measuring tool (especially in North America) and will help you be some-what precise in your cooking. However, as I mentioned earlier, when baking, I like weighing dry ingredients, as this improves the likelihood of even greater accuracy (and success!) of my recipes.

MEDIUM STAINLESS STEEL SAUCEPAN: The pan I own is 7 inches in diameter and I absolutely adore it. It is the perfect size for making sweet creams, jams, and vegan Nut-Free Ricotta (p. 264), and for melting chocolate over a double boiler. The fact that it is stainless steel allows me to use my metal whisk with it without fear of scratching off any nonstick coating.

MICROPLANE GRATER: Want my tip to making any dressing taste divine? Grate fresh garlic into it using a Microplane. It instantly elevates the dressing by highlighting the wonderful spiciness of the garlic. I also use it to grate ginger for stews, chocolate to use as garnish on desserts, and whole nutmeg—grating nutmeg right when you're using it helps ensure a fresh flavor.

MINI SILICONE SPATULAS: I cannot go a day without using one of my four mini spatulas! I use them for stirring sauces, creams, or anything remotely liquid. I also use them for scraping every little bit of batter out of mixing bowls and for getting into the nooks and crannies of my Vitamix blender. Although I also own large spatulas, I find that the mini ones come in handy more often in my day-to-day cooking and baking.

MORTAR AND PESTLE: I have struggled for years to find the perfect pepper grinder, and have a fear, perhaps irrational, that grinding pepper in my coffee grinder will taint the smell and taste of my morning elixir. Hence, I have come to use a mortar and pestle. Although it does take a little of elbow grease, I love that I can crush only as much pepper as I need for a recipe, thereby making sure it's extra fresh and potent.

MUFFIN PAN: A muffin pan is an essential when I'm making, well . . . muffins. Not only that, but I make scones in my muffin pan as well as mini cakes like my Piña Colada Cakes (p. 209). I suggest using one that is nonstick if you do not like using muffin liners.

PASTRY CUTTER: A pastry cutter is not essential for *everyone*; however, I own one and love it! I use it when making scones or a pastry crust for pies. I just really enjoy the act of manually incorporating the vegan butter with the dry ingredients. If you do not have one of these, don't stress it: a food processor will do the job too.

REMOVABLE-BOTTOM PIE PAN: Although I have to admit that I do not often use mine, I think the removable-bottom pie pan is a cool kitchen item to have when you want to make non-bake pies or Date-Sweetened Chocolate Cream Tarts (p. 231). You can either opt for a larger one (9 inches) or for four mini ones (5 inches each).

SERRATED KNIFE: Believe it or not, I lived the first 25 years of my life without touching a serrated knife. The day I purchased one upon the recommendation of Nisha Vora at Rainbow Plant Life, my life literally changed! Now I no longer *ever* struggle to cut a tomato or to slice (or should I say, squish!) a rustic loaf of bread. I hope you believe me when I say that a serrated knife is an absolute must in a kitchen. As with a chef's knife, be sure it is nice and sharp for optimal results.

SPRINGFORM CAKE PAN OR REGULAR CAKE PAN: I love using springform pans for most of my baking and find that I don't really need a regular cake pan. However, if you have only regular cake pans, those will do the trick for most of the recipes in this book. You will need 8- and 9-inch cake pans (springform or not). If you only have one of these, simply adjust your baking time accordingly (see my note on pan sizes on page 9).

WAFFLE IRON: When I turned twenty, I bought myself a waffle iron for my birthday. Not a fancy one, but one that had really good reviews and was reasonably priced. I have had it for over ten years now and I am so glad I treated myself all those years ago. For some reason, waffles feel like a treat to me. They are light, crispy, the perfect vehicle for maple syrup, and not much more complicated to make than pancakes. I have used my waffle iron for both sweet and savory waffles and would say it is one of my favorite kitchen appliances for whipping up a special weekend brunch.

WHISKS: I own three whisks: a mini one for dressings and for my Chocolate Microwave Cake of Your Dreams (p. 235)—I have one almost every week; don't judge! A medium one, slightly larger than the mini, for small quantities like sauces and creams. And a large one for whisking batter. Of course, you don't need all three, but I recommend owning at least a medium-sized one.

WOODEN SPOONS: Wooden spoons are my go-to utensil when cooking savory dishes in pans. Since they are not sensitive to heat, I can leave them in the pan without worrying that they will melt away. Also, these can be used with any kind of pot, as they do not scratch.

When I was growing up, the weekends were the time of the week that allowed my family to slow down, come together, and enjoy each other's company while indulging in some of our favorite foods.

On those slow mornings when my mom and I were able to spend a little extra time in the kitchen, we put together some of her classic breakfast dishes, which in turn inspired many recipes in this chapter. Through the years, as I grew my vegan food knowledge and explored trendy eats around the city and the world, I fell in love with recreating decadent brunches at home, which elevated our breakfast traditions.

Taking my time with weekend breakfasts is something I still do, now also sharing those cherished morning meals with my husband and his family. As you flip through this chapter, I encourage you to view each recipe as a treat for yourself or a loved one, an act of care and indulgence.

Bountiful Breakfasts

Strawberry Swirl Breakfast Muffins

(CUSTOMIZABLE) (EXTRA PREP)
(NUT/SEED-FREE)

MAKES: 12 MUFFINS
PREPARATION: 20 MINUTES
COOKING: 20 MINUTES

○ ○

2 cups (280 g) spelt flour

1 tsp baking powder

1 tsp baking soda

¼ tsp sea salt

¾ packed cup (5 oz/150 g)
    soft pitted dates (such as
    Bam or Medjool)

¾ cup (185 ml) water

½ cup (125 ml) unsweetened
    soy milk

¼ cup (60 ml) avocado oil

1 tsp apple cider vinegar

1 tsp vanilla extract

½ cup (125 ml) Date-Sweetened
    Chia Jam (p. 271), plus more
    for topping (see note)

Nut butter of choice, optional

○

SWEET BREAKFASTS ARE my *thing*. Although I have grown to love savory breakfasts, there is something incredibly comforting about starting the day off with a sweet dish. It feels like indulging in a dessert as your first meal of the day. Light to the touch, slightly moist, and featuring my fragrant Date-Sweetened Chia Jam (p. 271), these muffins are a wonderful way to enjoy a sweet breakfast that is not only nourishing but also completely naturally sweetened. As these muffins prove, granulated sugar–free does not mean flavor-free!

○ ○ ○

Preheat the oven to 350°F. Grease a muffin pan with cooking spray or avocado oil. Alternatively, you can line the pan with muffin liners.

In a large bowl, whisk together the spelt flour, baking powder, baking soda, and salt.

In a high-speed blender, blend the dates, water, soy milk, avocado oil, apple cider vinegar, and vanilla extract on high speed until smooth. Pour over the flour mixture. Whisk to combine.

Scoop 2 tablespoons of batter into each muffin cup. Repeat to fill 12 muffin cups. (You will have leftover batter at this point.) Top each muffin with ½ heaping tablespoon of jam. Top off with another tablespoon of batter. Use a toothpick to swirl the batter and jam together.

Bake for 17 to 20 minutes, until a toothpick inserted into the center comes out clean (it's okay if you notice some jam on the toothpick, just make sure you don't see raw batter on it). Let cool in the pan for 10 minutes, then transfer to a cooling rack and let cool completely.

Enjoy as is or with extra jam and nut butter, if desired. Store in the fridge in an airtight container for up to 4 days.

NOTE:

Feel free to use store-bought jam. If you're not really craving jam, leave it out and instead fold chocolate chips, chopped dried fruits, nuts, or seeds into the batter.

My Mom's Classic Crepes

(NUT/SEED-FREE)

MAKES: 12–14 CREPES
PREPARATION: 5 MINUTES
COOKING: 1 HOUR
RESTING: 15 MINUTES

2 cups (280 g) all-purpose flour

2 cup (500 ml) unsweetened
  soy milk

2 cups (500 ml) sparkling water

¼ cup (60 g) unsalted vegan
  butter, melted, plus more
  for greasing

2 tbsp (30 ml) maple syrup,
  plus more for serving

2 tsp vanilla extract (see note)

Mixed berries, for serving

Plant-based yogurt, for serving

Powdered sugar, for serving

WHEN I WAS growing up, crepes were one of my favorite breakfasts my mom would make (the other was French toast; find my take on page 65). The crepes would fill the kitchen with aromas of butter and vanilla, which felt like a culinary hug. My crepes are an adaptation of my mom's. They're vegan, of course, but they're just as supple, soft, and buttery! The secret ingredient here is sparkling water—it helps these crepes truly resemble the classic French crepe and its delightful lightness. If you're making these for my Grand Marnier Crepe Cake (p. 221) or Savory Stuffed Crepes (p. 197), follow the notes for each. Take your time with these: rather than starting with a burning hot pan, let the medium heat slowly cook each crepe to golden perfection (but watch the browning of the edges carefully, so they don't burn).

Sift the flour into a large bowl. Add the soy milk, sparkling water, melted butter, maple syrup, and vanilla extract (see note). Whisk until well combined—a few flour lumps are okay. Let sit until the batter has thickened, 15 minutes to 1 hour.

Preheat a 9-inch nonstick pan over medium heat (see note). Use a silicone brush to brush some butter onto the pan.

Whisk the batter a few times to smooth it out, then pour ⅓ cup of batter into the pan (or ¼ cup if making a tall Grand Marnier Crepe Cake; see note) and swirl it around to spread into a thin layer that nearly reaches the edges of the pan.

Cook for 2 to 3 minutes, until the edges start to pull away from the pan and the top looks dry. Flip and cook for another minute (see note). Transfer the crepe to a plate and cover with a clean kitchen towel to keep it warm and supple.

Repeat the process with the remaining batter, making sure to slightly butter the pan before adding the batter to prevent sticking and for extra decadence. If you notice that your crepes are getting too crispy, reduce the heat to medium-low.

CONTINUED ➤

Enjoy with fresh berries, yogurt, powdered sugar, and a drizzle of maple syrup.

Store the crepes in the fridge in an airtight container or on a plate tightly covered with foil for up to 2 days.

NOTES:

When making this recipe for my Savory Stuffed Crepes (p. 197), omit the vanilla extract.

If you want to cut your cooking time in half, use two pans instead of just one.

For a Grand Marnier Crepe Cake (p. 221) with more than 14 layers, use only ¼ cup of batter to form your crepes. However, if you are serving a bigger group, stick with ⅓ cup of batter, to make a wider cake, which will be easier to cut. Cover with a clean kitchen towel after preparing until ready to use.

Keep in mind, the first crepe is almost always the worst crepe. It might stick or be hard to flip. If, after your second crepe, you notice that your batter is too thick and does not spread well in the pan, add plant-based milk, 1 tablespoon (15 ml) at a time, until you reach a spreadable consistency. Alternatively, if your batter is too thin and sticks to the pan, add flour, 1 tablespoon (9 g) at a time.

Peaches and Cream Waffles

(NUT/SEED-FREE)

MAKES: 4 SERVINGS
PREPARATION: 10 MINUTES
COOKING: 30 MINUTES

WHEN I TURNED 20 years old, my gift to myself was a waffle iron—one that has helped me create dozens of brunches for my family through the years. For this recipe, I was inspired by the kind of waffles I'd order at a trendy Montreal brunch on an indulgent summer morning. Light and crispy on the outside, chewy and slightly buttery on the inside, they are the perfect vehicle for seasonal fruits, whipped cream, and a drizzle of maple syrup. Here, I've topped them with grilled-to-perfection peaches and coconut whipped cream. The sweet richness of the peaches complements the waffles' subtle vanilla and maple flavors. Summer is the best time to make these, when peaches are in season (and extra sweet and flavorful—and all the more so if you can get organic). That said, the waffles will go equally well with any of your favorite fruit.

2 cups (500 ml) unsweetened soy milk

2 tsp apple cider vinegar

2 cups (280 g) all-purpose flour (see note)

1½ tsp baking powder

¼ tsp sea salt

½ cup (115 g) melted unsalted vegan butter or refined coconut oil

¼ cup (60 ml) maple syrup

¼ cup (40 g) maple sugar

1 tbsp (15 ml) vanilla extract

In a bowl, whisk together the soy milk and apple cider vinegar. Let sit for 5 minutes.

Meanwhile, in large bowl, mix together the flour, baking powder, and salt.

Preheat the waffle iron. Preheat the oven to 200°F.

Add the melted butter, maple syrup, maple sugar, and vanilla extract to the soy milk mixture. Stir until the sugar is dissolved.

Pour the liquid mixture over the flour mixture and stir to incorporate.

If your waffle iron is not nonstick, grease the plates using melted butter, melted coconut oil, or cooking spray. If it is nonstick, there's no need to grease it.

Scoop about ½ cup of batter into the waffle iron. Close the waffle iron and cook until golden brown and crispy on both sides, about 5 minutes. Transfer to the oven to keep warm. Repeat the process with the remaining batter.

In a bowl, toss the peach slices with the melted butter to coat.

CONTINUED ➤

2 peaches, pitted and sliced
½ inch thick

2 tsp melted unsalted vegan butter,
plus more for the pan

2 tsp maple syrup, plus more
for serving

Pinch of sea salt

Coconut whipped cream,
sweetened with a pinch of
powdered sugar (I like to use Cha's
Organics' Coconut Whipping
Cream)

Heat a grill pan over medium-high heat, then grease with melted butter or coconut oil. Place the peach slices on the pan, reserving the bowl. Cook until grill marks appear, about 5 minutes. Flip and cook until grill marks appear on the other side.

Return the peaches to the bowl with the melted butter. Add the maple syrup and salt, and toss until coated.

Serve the waffles with the grilled peaches, coconut whipped cream, and maple syrup. Enjoy.

NOTES:

If you don't have maple sugar, use 2 tablespoons (30 g) of coconut sugar, granulated sugar, or organic cane sugar instead.

If you want to make these waffles a little more filling and fiber-richer, use half all-purpose flour and half whole-wheat flour.

NOTES:

Feeling extra fancy? Replace the nutritional yeast with 4 tablespoons (30 g) of your favorite shredded vegan cheese and omit the salt.

Basil, coriander, chives, dill, or parsley work great here in place of the sliced green onions.

Crispy Chickpea Pancakes with Avocado and Salsa

(CUSTOMIZABLE) (GLUTEN-FREE)
(NUT/SEED-FREE)

MAKES: FOUR 9-INCH PANCAKES
PREPARATION: 5 MINUTES
COOKING: 20 MINUTES
RESTING: 15 MINUTES

WHEN I FIRST became vegan, I gravitated toward sweet breakfasts, partly because there were fewer savory recipes online at the time. However, as I experimented in the kitchen, I discovered ingredients that could be easily incorporated into savory plant-based breakfasts, including chickpea flour. It's amazing in so many dishes, but one of my favorites is savory pancakes. They're simple and versatile, so after making this recipe as written, try it again with other ingredients. Have fun by folding in up to ⅓ cup of chopped veggies, or play around with various herbs to replace the green onions.

PANCAKE BATTER

1 cup (90 g) chickpea flour

1 cup (250 ml) water

1 tsp garlic powder

1 tsp sambal oelek or sriracha, optional

¼ tsp sea salt

Black pepper, to taste

3 tbsp (15 g) nutritional yeast (see note)

4 green onions, sliced (white and green parts), or ¼ cup chopped fresh herbs (see note)

2 tsp extra virgin olive oil

TOPPINGS

Bright Chopped Salsa (p. 266) or store-bought

Sliced avocado

Chili flakes, optional

Sliced green onions, optional (see note)

In a large bowl, whisk together the chickpea flour, water, garlic powder, sambal oelek, salt, and pepper.

Add the nutritional yeast and sliced green onions and stir. Let sit for 15 minutes.

Preheat the oven to 200°F. Line a baking sheet with parchment paper or a silicone mat.

Preheat a 9-inch nonstick frying pan or cast-iron skillet over medium-high heat. Use a silicone brush to evenly brush the skillet with ½ teaspoon of olive oil.

Give the batter a stir, then pour about ⅓ cup of it into the skillet and swirl the pan to spread the mixture fairly evenly.

Cook for 3 minutes or until the edges have browned up and the bottom of the pancake is brown in color.

Flip and cook for another 1 to 2 minutes, until lightly browned. Transfer to the prepared baking sheet and put in the oven to keep warm.

Reduce the stove heat to medium and repeat the process with the remaining batter, greasing the pan with ½ teaspoon of olive oil each time.

Enjoy with the salsa, sliced avocado, chili flakes, and more green onions, if desired.

Whole-Wheat Banana Bread Pancakes

(NUT/SEED-FREE)

MAKES: 14–16 PANCAKES
PREPARATION: 10 MINUTES
COOKING: 30 MINUTES

I DID NOT grow up eating pancakes. It was only when we arrived in Canada that I discovered American-style pancakes. Now they are one of my favorite breakfasts to make when I have a little extra time on my hands in the morning (nope, I am not the kind of person who whips pancakes up on a random Monday morning!). For a while, I hesitated between sharing a banana bread recipe in this cookbook and sharing a pancake recipe. Because there are so many variations of both, I settled for a recipe that married both of those classics. These thick and decadent pancakes are made with whole-wheat flour (to keep you full for longer!) and feature mashed bananas, along with decadent vegan chocolate chips and chopped banana chips (which are optional, but they add a nice chewiness and texture that I love). This recipe is a great one to kick-start the weekend.

○ ○

1½ cups (210 g) whole-wheat flour

1 tbsp (12 g) baking powder

½ tsp ground cinnamon

¼ tsp sea salt

1 cup + 2 tbsp (280 ml) unsweetened soy milk

½ cup (120 g) mashed banana

2 packed tbsp (1 oz/25 g) soft pitted dates or 2 tbsp (30 ml) maple syrup (see note)

2 tbsp (30 g) melted unsalted vegan butter, plus more for greasing

½ cup (70 g) vegan chocolate chips (see note, p. 44), plus more for serving

½ cup (50 g) crushed banana chips, plus more for serving, optional

Banana slices, for serving

Maple syrup, for serving

○ ○ ○

In a large bowl, mix together the whole-wheat flour, baking powder, cinnamon, and salt.

In a blender, blend the soy milk, mashed banana, dates, and melted butter on high speed until smooth. Pour the banana mixture into the bowl with the flour mixture. Mix with a wooden spoon until fully combined.

Fold in the chocolate chips and crushed banana chips, if using. The batter will be very fluffy and thick.

Preheat the oven to 200°F.

Heat a large pan over medium heat. Use a silicone brush to evenly brush the pan with melted butter, then spoon 2 tablespoons of batter into the pan. Use the back of a spoon to carefully flatten the batter in the pan—because the batter is thick, you most likely won't be able to form a perfect circle. Depending on the size of your pan, you should be able to fit between 2 and 3 pancakes in the pan.

Cook until the pancakes puff up, their edges are dry, and the bottoms are golden brown. Flip the pancakes and cook for another minute or until golden brown on the bottom.

CONTINUED ➤

Transfer the cooked pancakes to a baking sheet or an ovenproof serving plate and keep warm in the oven while you prepare the remaining pancakes.

To serve, top the pancakes with sliced bananas, chocolate chips, crushed banana chips, and a drizzle of maple syrup.

Store leftovers in the fridge in separate airtight containers for up to 2 days.

NOTES:

If you use maple syrup instead of dates, there's no need to blend the liquid ingredients together; you can just whisk them together in a bowl, making sure no big banana clumps remain.

I prefer to use 70% chocolate chips, but opt for what you have on hand—or you could fold chopped dark chocolate into the batter.

Savory Cornmeal and Green Onion Waffles

(GLUTEN-FREE)　(NUT/SEED-FREE)

MAKES: 4–6 WAFFLES
PREPARATION: 15 MINUTES
COOKING: 30 MINUTES

GOLDEN, SAVORY WAFFLES topped with a luxurious vegan hollandaise sauce, vegan sausage, chopped jalapeños, and a touch of greenery—all made at home. Yes, you read that right, and you can do it too! I wanted these waffles to be reminiscent of cornbread, without being too heavy, so I've made the batter from a mixture of cornmeal and gluten-free flour, adding subtle flavor and a tender texture with the green onion. Although not using as much butter as traditional hollandaise, my version is still rich and creamy, a result of using silken tofu. It also uses black salt (kala namak), for that classic eggy hollandaise flavor. There are a few more steps to this recipe than for a traditional waffle recipe; I like to think of each one as a flavor building block, bringing you one step closer to a dish worthy of an epic weekend brunch.

○ ○

WAFFLES

1 cup (140 g) fine polenta
(#400 fine cornmeal)

1 cup (150 g) gluten-free flour
(I like Bob's Red Mill Gluten-Free 1-to-1 Baking Flour)

2 tbsp (10 g) nutritional yeast

1½ tsp baking powder

1 tbsp (6 g) dried chopped onion

1 tsp garlic powder

1 tsp sea salt

½ tsp black pepper

1 cup (250 ml) unsweetened soy milk

½ cup (125 ml) extra virgin olive oil

1 tbsp (15 ml) maple syrup

4 green onions (green and white parts), sliced

○ ○ ○

PREPARE THE WAFFLES

Preheat the waffle iron. Preheat the oven to 200°F.

In a large bowl, mix together the cornmeal, gluten-free flour, nutritional yeast, baking powder, dried chopped onion, garlic powder, salt, and pepper.

Mix in the soy milk, olive oil, and maple syrup until well incorporated. Use a silicone spatula to fold in the green onions.

If your waffle iron is not nonstick, grease the plates using avocado oil or cooking spray. If it is nonstick, there's no need to grease it.

Scoop about ½ cup of batter into the waffle iron. Close the waffle iron and cook until golden and crispy on both sides, about 5 minutes. Transfer the waffle to a baking sheet or ovenproof serving plate. Place in the oven to keep warm. Repeat the process with the remaining batter.

CONTINUED ➤

HOLLANDAISE

1 (10 oz/300 g) package silken tofu, drained

2 tbsp (10 g) nutritional yeast

1 tbsp (15 ml) lemon juice

1 tsp black salt (kala namak)

¼ tsp turmeric (see note)

¼ cup (125 ml) water

Pinch of cayenne pepper, plus more to taste

Pinch of black pepper, plus more to taste

Sea salt, to taste

1 tbsp (15 g) melted unsalted vegan butter

TOPPINGS

4 vegan sausages (I like Gusta sausages best)

1–2 chopped jalapeños (see note)

2 sliced green onions, green and white parts

½ cup microgreens

Black pepper

PREPARE THE HOLLANDAISE

In a blender, blend all the ingredients except the melted butter on medium speed. With the motor running, slowly pour in the melted butter, blending until smooth. Taste and adjust seasonings to your liking.

PREPARE THE TOPPINGS AND SERVE

Cook the vegan sausages in a pan set over medium heat until they are browned and caramelized. You might need to add some neutral cooking oil (such as avocado, canola, or melted refined coconut) to the pan to prevent them from sticking.

Warm up the hollandaise by transferring it to a saucepan and heating over low heat, stirring often. If the sauce forms little clumps, simply blend it again before serving or use an immersion blender to blend everything together.

Serve the waffles topped with slices of vegan sausage, a drizzle of hollandaise sauce, chopped jalapeños, sliced green onions, microgreens, and a crack of pepper.

Store leftovers in the fridge in separate airtight containers. The waffles can be stored for up to 2 days; the hollandaise can be stored for up to 1 week; and the vegan sausage can be stored for up to 3 days. Reheat the waffles, hollandaise, and vegan sausage before enjoying.

NOTES:

The color of the hollandaise will become more vibrant as it cooks, but if you want it to be an even deeper yellow, add an extra ⅛ teaspoon of turmeric.

For a milder brunch, cut the jalapeños in half lengthwise and remove the seeds before chopping.

Leftover hollandaise can be warmed up and used in vegan eggs Benedict or a breakfast poutine.

Stewed Blackberries and Lemon Ricotta Toasts

(CUSTOMIZABLE)

(GLUTEN-FREE OPTION)

(NUT/SEED-FREE) (EXTRA PREP)

MAKES: 2 LARGE OR 4 SMALL
  TOASTS
PREPARATION: 10 MINUTES
COOKING: 20 MINUTES

∘ ∘

STEWED BLACKBERRIES

1 heaping cup (6 oz/170 g)
  blackberries

1 tbsp maple syrup

1 tbsp lemon juice

LEMONY RICOTTA

¼ cup Nut-Free Ricotta (p. 264)

2 tsp maple syrup

Zest of ½ a lemon

1 tsp lemon juice

2 large or 4 small slices of good-
  quality bread

Unsalted vegan butter, optional
  but recommended for toasting

∘

UPON TRYING THIS DISH for the first time, my husband said, "This tastes like cheesecake on toast." I could not find a better way to describe it! The best part about this recipe is that if you already have my Nut-Free Ricotta (p. 264) on hand, all you need to do is to focus on slowly cooking the fragrant blackberries to perfection before serving. This buttery toasted bread topped with rich, creamy, lemony homemade ricotta and garnished with juicy blackberries may very well make you feel as if you're treating yourself at a trendy vegan restaurant.

∘ ∘ ∘

PREPARE THE BLACKBERRIES

In a small saucepan, lightly stir together the blackberries, maple syrup, and lemon juice. Cover and cook over medium heat for 10 minutes, stirring once halfway through the cooking time. Remove the lid and cook for another 5 minutes. Remove from the heat and let cool in the pan for 5 minutes while you prepare the ricotta spread.

PREPARE THE LEMONY RICOTTA

In a bowl, combine the Nut-Free Ricotta, maple syrup, lemon zest, and lemon juice.

Toast the bread right before serving (see note). Spread 2 tablespoons of lemony ricotta on each piece of toast and dollop with the stewed blackberries. When spooning on the berries, try to leave behind as much of their juices as possible, to avoid soaking the bread. Enjoy.

NOTES:

An extra decadent toasting method is to spread ¼ to ½ teaspoon of unsalted butter onto each slice of bread and toast in a pan (or grill pan) over medium-high heat, 2 to 3 minutes per side.

Instead of using blackberries, try halved or quartered strawberries (think strawberry cheesecake!).

Herby Mushroom and Ricotta Toasts

(CUSTOMIZABLE)

(GLUTEN-FREE OPTION)

(NUT/SEED-FREE)   (EXTRA PREP)

MAKES: 2 LARGE OR
   4 SMALL TOASTS
PREPARATION: 5 MINUTES
COOKING: 15 MINUTES

WHEN I TRAVEL, I plan my days around where I will eat. When my husband and I traveled to Vancouver, we sought out brunch at TurF. I tried their mushroom-ricotta toast and I fell in love! It had *the perfect* level of creaminess and herby umami flavor. My version is nut-free and easy to customize: switch up the herbs with whatever you're feeling or have handy. Even the star ingredient can be played with: button and cremini mushrooms work, but I prefer a mix of cremini, oyster, and king oyster to add more depth. Most importantly, don't rush the mushroom's caramelization. This is when the flavor develops, so refrain from constantly stirring, and don't hesitate to increase the heat. Now, have fun and enjoy life-changing mushrooms!

UMAMI MUSHROOMS

1 tbsp avocado oil

½ large onion, diced

3 cups sliced mushrooms of choice

1 tbsp fresh thyme, plus more
   for garnish

1 garlic clove, minced

1 tbsp + 2 tsp tamari

¼ tsp black pepper, plus more
   for garnish

GARLICKY RICOTTA

¼ cup Nut-Free Ricotta (p. 264)

½ tsp garlic powder

½ tsp lemon juice

Pinch of sea salt

2 large or 4 small slices of good-
   quality bread

Unsalted vegan butter, optional
   but recommended for toasting

Heat the avocado oil in a large pan set over medium-high heat. Add the onions and mushrooms and cook until golden and caramelized, stirring occasionally to keep from burning. Do not hesitate to increase the heat to help the water evaporate and the mushrooms brown.

Reduce the heat to medium. Add the thyme, garlic, tamari, and pepper. Cook for another minute or until the tamari is absorbed. Remove from the heat.

Make the garlicky ricotta by combining all its ingredients in a bowl.

Right before serving, toast the bread (see note on page 53).

Spread 2 tablespoons of garlicky ricotta onto each toast and top with the herby mushrooms. Garnish with more thyme and pepper and enjoy.

Chocolate Cardamom Oat-Free Granola

(CUSTOMIZABLE)

(GLUTEN-FREE OPTION)

(NUT/SEED-FREE OPTION)

MAKES: 4 CUPS
PREPARATION: 10 MINUTES
COOKING: 25 MINUTES

WHEN I FIRST became vegan, I ate homemade granola almost daily on smoothie bowls and very often on its own, straight out of the jar. Upon realizing that my skin was not tolerating oats and many nuts very well, I thought I had to give up granola. Until, that is, I made this alternative to oat-based granola! This version is flavored with aromatic cardamom and cocoa—*plus,* dark chocolate is sprinkled on while the granola is still hot, giving an extra depth of flavor and making it extra decadent. Perfect eaten on its own, with plant-based milk, or as a topping on smoothie bowls or vegan ice cream sundaes, this granola is a wonderful pantry staple to have on hand when you are craving a little something crunchy. It is now part of my Sunday food-prep ritual to make a batch of this granola to enjoy throughout the week, as a little daily luxurious snack.

---

3 cups (45 g) puffed wheat cereal (see note)

1 cup (30 g) unflavored Rice Chex cereal

1 cup (20 g) puffed quinoa

½ cup (60 g) raw pepitas, optional (see note)

2 tbsp (20 g) ground flax or chia seeds

3 tbsp (15 g) Dutch-processed cocoa powder

1½ tsp ground cardamom

½ tsp instant coffee powder, optional

¼ tsp sea salt

⅓ cup (80 ml) maple syrup

¼ cup (60 ml) avocado oil or canola oil

1 tsp vanilla extract

2 tbsp (30 g) finely chopped dark chocolate

Preheat the oven to 300°F. Line a baking sheet with parchment paper or a silicone mat.

In a large bowl, toss together the puffed wheat, Rice Chex, puffed quinoa, pepitas, ground flax, cocoa powder, cardamom, instant coffee, and salt, using a silicone spatula to distribute everything evenly.

Pour in the maple syrup, avocado oil, and vanilla extract. Stir to coat. Transfer to the prepared baking sheet and bake for 15 minutes, then use the spatula to toss the granola before baking for another 10 minutes.

Remove from the oven and immediately sprinkle the chopped dark chocolate over the hot granola.

Let cool completely before transferring to an airtight container. Store at room temperature for up to 2 weeks.

NOTES:

This recipe is very customizable! Use the puffed cereals of your choice—kamut and rice are great alternatives. If you avoid gluten, use a mixture of puffed quinoa, puffed rice, and gluten-free Rice Chex. Rice Chex cereal can be replaced with more puffed cereals if you prefer less-processed cereal.

If you eat nuts or seeds, you can absolutely use ½ cup of your choice of those instead or combined with the pepitas, just be sure to chop them up first.

Creamy Coconut Rice Pudding

(GLUTEN-FREE) (NUT/SEED-FREE)

MAKES: 4–6 SERVINGS
PREPARATION: 5 MINUTES
COOKING: 40 MINUTES
RESTING: 15 MINUTES

MY MOM'S *riz au lait* (rice pudding) was synonymous with comfort when I was young. Whereas she used precooked rice with milk, butter, and sugar, my take is a little different but just as comforting. I use arborio rice, which becomes wonderfully creamy and chewy as it cooks while keeping its shape. This type of rice requires a little extra attention and love: slowly cooking it in rich and decadent coconut milk before it's brought together with the flavor boosters and thickening agent. This recipe is in the book's breakfast section, but, really, you could have this pudding any time of the day, and even eat it chilled—I particularly love it as a cold dessert.

1½ cups unsweetened soy milk

1 (13½ oz/400 ml) can full-fat coconut milk (see note)

½ cup arborio rice

3 tbsp maple syrup, plus more to taste

½ tsp cornstarch

¼ tsp ground cinnamon, plus more for garnish, optional

Pinch of sea salt

1 tsp vanilla extract (see note)

Chopped pistachios, for garnish, optional

In a saucepan, bring the soy milk and coconut milk to a boil, uncovered, about 10 minutes. Keep an eye on the mixture, stirring often with a silicone spatula to prevent it from boiling over.

Reduce the heat to low and add the arborio rice. Cook until the rice is soft, about 25 minutes, stirring every 5 minutes or so. Use a spoon to scoop out the thin film that forms.

Meanwhile, in a small bowl, whisk together the maple syrup, cornstarch, cinnamon, and salt.

Once the rice is soft, pour the maple mixture into the saucepan. Stir, then increase the heat to high. Continue cooking for 1 to 3 minutes, until the mixture has thickened, stirring constantly to prevent it from sticking to the bottom of the pan. Taste and add the vanilla extract and more maple syrup to your liking.

Remove from the heat and let cool in the pan for 15 minutes to help the mixture thicken further before enjoying as is or sprinkled with cinnamon and chopped pistachios. Store the leftovers in the fridge in an airtight container for up to 3 days (see note).

NOTES:

You can swap out the canned coconut milk with 1⅔ cups of unsweetened coconut beverage, but keep in mind that this will make your rice pudding a little less rich.

For a more floral pudding, replace the vanilla extract with ½ teaspoon of orange blossom water.

If eating this pudding cold, cool to room temperature before chilling.

NOTES:

If you are making the bacon the same day as these sandwiches, start off by marinating it. Then place the slices on the baking sheet along with the hash browns.

Add your own flair to this sandwich by incorporating sliced pickles, basil, sun-dried tomato pesto, or even store-bought cooked vegan eggs (such as JUST Egg).

Ultimate Breakfast Sandwich

(CUSTOMIZABLE)

(GLUTEN-FREE OPTION)

(NUT/SEED-FREE) (EXTRA PREP)

MAKES: 2 SANDWICHES
PREPARATION: 10 MINUTES
COOKING: 30 MINUTES

FUN FACT: I've never loved breakfast sandwiches or fast-food hash browns, even before going vegan. However, I slowly began liking them when I met Sam, who is an absolute fan of everything breakfast, and has a very special place in his heart for breakfast sandwiches and hash browns. I created this elevated comfort-food breakfast sandwich especially for him. Yes, the bread is a humble English muffin, but layered inside are a crispy hash brown, a slightly spicy spread, creamy mashed avocado, a touch of greens, homemade smoky Tofu Bacon (p. 59), and bright and tangy Pickled Onions (p. 267). To help the flavors and textures reach new heights, allow your hash browns the time to really crisp up in the oven. You want them to be closer to caramel rather than light honey in color. This sandwich is for the breakfast sandwich lovers out there and for all those who love reinventing classics in the kitchen.

2 store-bought frozen hash browns

2 tbsp Homemade Mayo (p. 258) or store-bought vegan mayonnaise

2 tsp sambal oelek or sriracha

1 small ripe avocado, peeled and pitted

Sea salt and black pepper, to taste

Small squeeze of lemon juice

2 English muffins, regular, whole-wheat, or gluten-free

2 leaves of curly lettuce

8 slices of Tofu Bacon (p. 59) (see note)

Pickled Onions (p. 267)

Preheat the oven to 425°F. Line a baking sheet with parchment paper or a silicone mat.

Place the hash browns on the prepared baking sheet and bake for 25 minutes or until deep brown in color—you are looking for them to have a very crunchy exterior.

Prepare the spicy mayo in a small bowl by mixing together the mayo and sambal oelek. Taste and add more sambal oelek if you are looking for a spicier spread.

In a separate small bowl, mash the avocado with a fork. Season it with a pinch each of salt and pepper. Stir in the lemon juice to prevent the avocado from browning. Set aside.

Two minutes before removing the hash browns from the oven, slice the English muffins in half and toast them in the oven for 2 minutes.

Assemble the sandwiches by spreading about 2 teaspoons of spicy mayo on each English muffin half. Top 2 halves with the crispy hash browns, lettuce, 4 slices of tofu bacon per sandwich, mashed avocado, and pickled onions. Top with the remaining 2 muffin halves and enjoy.

Tofu Bacon

GLUTEN-FREE NUT/SEED-FREE

MAKES: ABOUT 16 SLICES
PREPARATION: 10 MINUTES
COOKING: 25 MINUTES
RESTING: 15 MINUTES

I HAVE TRIED making all kinds of vegan bacon in my life: versions made with eggplant, tempeh, mushrooms, crumbled tofu, and so much more! Every variation has its place and purpose, in my opinion—that is what I love about vegan cuisine. I created this recipe because I wanted a bacon imitation that was chewy, dense, and slightly crispy all at once. Slicing the tofu thinly and baking it at a high temperature allows a lot of the water in it to evaporate, so the tofu becomes delightfully chewy, while also having really crispy edges. The mixture of spices all work together to infuse this plant-based bacon with lots of flavor, making it a delicious brunch side dish or a star in my Ultimate Breakfast Sandwich (p. 57). For extra smoky, spicy, and garlicky flavor, make sure to take a few extra minutes to ensure the tofu is well coated with the marinade, and if you can, allow time do its magic and marinate the bacon overnight.

2 tbsp tamari

1 tbsp maple syrup

1 tbsp avocado oil

1 tsp smoked paprika

½ tsp sweet paprika

½ tsp chili powder

¼ tsp garlic powder

½ lb (227 g) extra-firm tofu

In a large container with a lid, mix together the tamari, maple syrup, avocado oil, both paprikas, chili powder, and garlic powder.

Thinly slice the block of tofu crosswise, creating slices of about ⅛ to ¹⁄₁₀ inch thick. Do not worry if some of the pieces break a little bit, just try your best to make them all about the same thickness to prevent some from burning when in the oven.

Place the tofu slices in the marinating liquid and seal the container. Flip the container upside down and then right side up, to coat the tofu in the marinade somewhat evenly. Don't do this too fast or the tofu may break.

Marinate for at least 15 minutes and up to 24 hours. If marinating for more than an hour, place in the fridge.

Preheat the oven to 425°F. Line a baking sheet with parchment paper or a silicone mat.

Place the tofu slices on the prepared baking sheet. Bake for 20 to 25 minutes, until the tofu bacon has shrunk slightly and the sides have crisped up.

Remove from the oven and enjoy as a side for brunch or in my Ultimate Breakfast Sandwich (p. 57). Store in the fridge in an airtight container for up to 5 days. Reheat it in the microwave on high power for 15 to 30 seconds or until warm.

Rum-Coconut French Toast with Caramelized Bananas

(GLUTEN-FREE OPTION)

(NUT/SEED-FREE) (EXTRA PREP)

MAKES: 8–10 SLICES
PREPARATION: 15 MINUTES
COOK TIME: 30 MINUTES
RESTING: 8 HOURS

○ FRENCH TOAST WAS ONE of my mom's fancier go-to breakfast recipes when I was growing up. We would call it *pain perdu* (lost bread), and all of us kids just loved it when my mom made a fresh batch on the weekend. My version is inspired by both my mom (who first introduced me to this breakfast classic) and a French toast recipe I saw Bobby Flay make on TV that requires overnight refrigeration and features thick, rustic bread. Instead of eggs, I use cornstarch to thicken the liquid mixture, as well as nutritional yeast to add a little savory flavor. Because the bread slices soak up the liquid overnight, the French toast ends up almost custard-like on the inside, with a golden, slightly crispy exterior. This version is extra special, as it features delightful coconut and rum flavors, and is served with soft, gooey, rum-flavored caramelized bananas and coconut flakes.

○ ○

FRENCH TOAST

2 tbsp cornstarch

1 tbsp nutritional yeast

1 tsp ground cinnamon

1 cup full-fat coconut milk (see note)

1 cup water

¼ cup maple syrup

2 tbsp brown rum

1 tsp vanilla extract

8–10 slices (¾ inch thick) of crusty bread, such as sourdough or country-style boule

All-purpose flour, for dusting

Extra virgin coconut oil, for cooking

○ ○ ○

In a large bowl, whisk together the cornstarch, nutritional yeast, and cinnamon.

Whisk in the coconut milk, water, maple syrup, rum, and vanilla extract. Submerge the slices of bread in the coconut milk mixture one at a time, letting each soak it up for 10 seconds, then transfer to a large baking dish, laying them in a single layer.

Pour any remaining liquid over the bread, then cover the bread with foil. Refrigerate for at least 8 hours and up to 24 hours.

The next day, preheat the oven to 200°F and line a baking sheet with parchment paper or a silicone mat.

Lightly dust the bread with flour; I use about ¼ teaspoon per slice.

In a nonstick pan set over medium heat, melt about ½ teaspoon of coconut oil, spreading it evenly in the pan with a silicone brush. Place 2 to 3 slices of soaked bread in the pan, floured side down, and cook until golden brown, about 2 to 3 minutes.

CONTINUED ➤

CARAMELIZED BANANAS

2 tbsp unsalted vegan butter

2 bananas, peeled and sliced
   ½ inch thick

2 tbsp maple syrup

1 tsp brown rum

Pinch of sea salt

Coconut flakes, for garnish

Maple syrup, for serving

Lightly dust more flour overtop the bread. If you find that the pan is getting so hot that the bread is starting to burn, reduce the heat to medium-low.

Flip the bread and cook for an additional 2 to 3 minutes, then place on the prepared baking sheet and transfer to the oven to keep warm.

Repeat with the remaining slices of bread, keeping the cooked slices warm in the oven.

Wipe the pan clean. Melt the butter in the pan set over medium heat.

Add the banana slices and cook for 2 to 3 minutes, until brown, then flip and cook on the other side until golden brown and caramelized.

Drizzle in the maple syrup and rum and cook for 2 more minutes, gently stirring, or until the bananas have caramelized and the maple syrup has thickened and coated them.

Sprinkle the bananas with a pinch of salt.

Serve the warm French toast topped with the caramelized bananas, coconut flakes, and a drizzle of maple syrup.

NOTE:

You can use 2 cups of light coconut milk or coconut beverage from a carton instead of 1 cup of full-fat coconut milk and 1 cup of water.

No-Knead Overnight Dutch Oven Bread

(CUSTOMIZABLE) (NUT/SEED-FREE)
(EXTRA PREP)

MAKES: 1 LOAF
PREPARATION: 10 MINUTES
COOKING: 35 MINUTES
RESTING: 8–12 HOURS

DREAMING OF HOMEMADE BREAD that requires no kneading and very little intervention? Well, you are in luck. This recipe is an adaptation of one from the blogger Jenny Jones, of the Jenny Can Cook blog, and has become a go-to in my household. Every Sunday, Sam and I set aside some time at the end of the day to prepare the dough for a loaf or two of bread, letting the yeast and air do its magic overnight, then following a few simple steps the next day so we've got our homemade bread for the week. I love that this recipe requires few ingredients and is customizable. Before you ask: yes, you do need a Dutch oven for this recipe, and let me tell you, if you want to get into making easy breads at home, you will not regret purchasing one if you don't already have one. This bread is chewy yet with a lovely crispy crust, and once you get the hang of the steps, you'll see how easy it is to make!

○ ○

2 cups (280 g) whole-wheat flour

1 cup (120 g) bread flour or
   1 cup (140 g) all-purpose flour
   (see note)

1 tbsp (15 g) organic cane sugar

½ tsp sea salt

¼ tsp instant yeast

1½ cups (375 ml) room-
   temperature water (straight
   from the tap works)

○ ○ ○

In a large bowl, place the whole-wheat flour, bread flour, sugar, salt, and instant yeast. Stir with a wooden spoon or a silicone spatula.

Add the water and mix to incorporate. You can use your spoon to help form a somewhat uniform ball of dough. No need to knead the dough or make it perfectly smooth; it will all come together with time.

Cover the bowl with plastic wrap and then with a clean kitchen towel, and put in a warm place for 8 to 12 hours to allow the dough to rise.

Dust a clean work surface with flour and transfer the dough to it. Lightly dust the dough with flour. Using your hands or a flexible dough scraper, form a ball with the dough.

Line the bowl with parchment paper, allowing it to come up the sides of the bowl. (You can first line it with the plastic wrap, if you like; see note.)

Transfer the ball of dough to the parchment-lined bowl. Cover with a clean kitchen towel and let rise for 30 minutes.

CONTINUED ➤

Meanwhile, place the Dutch oven with its lid on in the oven and preheat the oven to 450°F. After 30 minutes, carefully remove the hot Dutch oven and remove the lid. Remove the towel covering the dough. Hold the corners of the parchment paper to lift the dough and transfer it (along with the parchment paper) to the hot Dutch oven. Cover with the lid and bake for 30 minutes.

Remove the bread from the Dutch oven and place directly on the oven rack (without the parchment paper). Bake for 2 to 5 minutes, to create a beautiful brown crust all around it.

Remove from the oven and let cool completely before slicing.

Store at room temperature in a large zip-seal bag for up to 1 week.

Enjoy as you prefer or with my Herby Mushroom and Ricotta Toasts (p. 50) or Stewed Blackberries and Lemon Ricotta Toasts (p. 49).

NOTES:

I like lining my bowl with plastic wrap before lining it with parchment paper to avoid getting any leftover dough on the bottom and sides of the parchment paper (that way there's no need to wash the Dutch oven after baking), but you can clean the bowl first and then line it directly with parchment paper, if you prefer.

Wanting 100% whole-wheat bread? No problem! Just replace the 1 cup (120 g) of bread flour with 1 cup (140 g) of whole-wheat flour. Wanting a lighter, white loaf? Use 3 cups (360 g) of bread or all-purpose flour, omitting the whole-wheat flour.

What about add-ins?

○ *Feel free to fold ½ cup (60 g) of your favorite nuts and seeds into the dough before leaving it to rise overnight. If using larger nuts like almonds, walnuts, pecans, cashews, and pistachios, chop before folding in.*

○ *Looking for a sweeter loaf? Replace the 1½ (375 ml) cup of water with ¼ cup (60 ml) of maple syrup and just 1¼ cups (310 ml) of water, plus add 1½ teaspoons of ground cinnamon, and 1½ cup (50 g) of raisins to the dough. Omit the final step of browning for 5 minutes on the oven rack.*

Savory Breakfast Scones

(CUSTOMIZABLE) (NUT/SEED-FREE)

YIELD: 8 SCONES
PREPARATION: 10 MINUTES
COOKING: 40 MINUTES
RESTING: 30 MINUTES

WHEN I THINK OF my ultimate brunch, baked goods are always a part of it. Scones are probably one of my favorite brunch items, simply because they're incredibly versatile. The base dough for this recipe is one I developed years ago and adapt for every scone recipe I create. For these savory scones, I use less sugar and vegan butter than for my usual sweet scone recipe, because vegan cheese and sausage are folded in. One key to making these scones a success is to use *flavored* vegan sausage—whether it's Italian, spicy Italian, smoked, or Mexican, your scones will be infused with extra flavor. This recipe is one you can really have fun with. Get creative and play around with the add-ins by modifying them to your liking and based on what you have or are craving.

1 tbsp (15 ml) olive oil, plus more for brushing

1 shallot (40 g), finely diced

1 packed cup (200 g) flavored vegan sausage crumbled into chunks

2 garlic cloves, minced

¾ cup (185 ml) unsweetened soy milk

1 tsp apple cider vinegar

1½ cups (210 g) all-purpose flour

½ cup (70 g) whole-wheat flour

2 tbsp (30 g) organic cane sugar

1½ tsp baking powder

½ tsp sea salt

⅓ cup (25 g) nutritional yeast

6 tbsp (90 g) cold unsalted vegan butter, cubed

½ cup (60 g) shredded vegan cheese

½ cup (35 g) sliced green onions or chives, green and white parts

In a nonstick pan, heat the olive oil over medium heat. Add the shallots and cook for 2 minutes or until golden.

Add the sausage and cook for 3 to 5 minutes, until brown and caramelized. Break up any bigger chunks of sausage using a wooden spoon.

Sprinkle in the minced garlic and cook for 30 seconds or until fragrant. Transfer the mixture to a bowl and cool in the fridge for 10 minutes.

Meanwhile, in a small bowl, mix together the soy milk and apple cider vinegar. Let sit for 5 minutes to curdle slightly.

In a large bowl, sift together the all-purpose flour, whole-wheat flour, sugar, baking powder, and salt. If there is bran left in the sifter after sifting the whole-wheat flour, add it to the bowl. Stir in the nutritional yeast using a silicone spatula.

Add the butter and incorporate it, using a pastry cutter or a fork, until the mixture forms a soft, sandy texture that slightly sticks together when pinched. Alternatively, in a food processor, pulse together the dry ingredients, then pulse in the butter. Transfer the mixture to a large bowl before moving onto the next step.

CONTINUED ➤

Add the cheese, green onions, and cooled sausage mixture to the flour mixture. Stir to combine, then stir in the soy milk mixture using a silicone spatula.

Use your hands to form the dough into a ball. Wrap the dough in plastic wrap and refrigerate for 30 minutes. (Do not skip this step! It helps slightly harden the butter back up, making for flakier scones.)

Preheat the oven to 375°F. Line a baking sheet with parchment paper or a silicone mat.

Lightly dust a clean work surface with flour and place the dough on it.

Lightly dust a rolling pin with flour, then roll the dough into a circle 9 inches in diameter. Use your hands to round the edges. Cut the circle in half, then cut each half into 4 pieces, giving you 8 scones in total. Brush each scone with a bit of olive oil.

Transfer the scones to the prepared baking sheet and bake for 25 to 30 minutes, until golden brown. To add a bit of extra color to your scones, broil at 500°F for 1 to 2 minutes, until they gain a deeper brown color.

Remove from the oven and let cool on a cooling rack for 10 minutes before enjoying.

Store at room temperature in an airtight container for up to 3 days. Reheat the scones in the oven at 400°F for 1 to 2 minutes, then enjoy.

NOTES:

There are so many add-ins you could try, such as:

° *Chopped sun-dried tomatoes, slightly patted dry with paper towel before folding in*

° *Finely chopped red bell pepper, cooked along with the shallot-sausage mixture or folded in raw*

° *Chopped vegan bacon (cooked along with the sausage mixture)*

° *Chopped fresh herbs like thyme, oregano, chives, and parsley*

° *Chopped pitted black or Kalamata olives*

If you want to make these scones in advance, you can refrigerate the dough overnight.

Tangawis

(GLUTEN-FREE) (NUT/SEED-FREE)

(EXTRA PREP)

MAKES: 4 CUPS
PREPARATION: 5 MINUTES
RESTING: 24 HOURS

○ THERE ARE TWO DRINKS I remember from my childhood in Congo: Grenadine and Tangawis. Grenadine is a bright red and sweet sparkling drink made of grenadine syrup, while Tangawis is a yellowish-beige juice made from fresh ginger. I remember it being very bright in flavor, spicy, and so refreshing. It is only through writing this book that I attempted making the recipe for myself, and through the testing process, I have reconnected with this beloved childhood drink. My favorite step in making this recipe is straining the elixir through a nut milk bag, releasing all that bright goodness from the ginger. Although this drink is made with only four ingredients, you can have fun experimenting with the flavoring by adding more maple syrup or citrus juice, for instance. You can even incorporate it in cocktails! I never drink more than ⅓ cup of it at a time because it is very concentrated.

○ ○

1 cup peeled and chopped organic ginger (see note)

3½ cups water

3 tbsp maple syrup (see note)

2 tbsp lime juice or lemon juice (see note)

○ ○ ○

In a high-speed blender, blend the ginger and water on high speed for 30 seconds. Transfer the mixture to a 32-oz mason jar and discard the ginger pulp. Seal the jar with its lid and refrigerate for 24 hours.

The next day, shake the jar for 10 seconds, then set a nut milk bag (see note) into a mixing bowl large enough to hold 4 cups of liquid. Pour the ginger mixture into the bag, twist the top of the bag, and squeeze it to extract the juice from the ginger flesh.

Use a silicone spatula or a whisk to stir in the maple syrup and lime juice. Taste and adjust the sweetness and acidity levels as desired.

Give the jar a rinse, then pour the ginger juice back into it. Store the juice in the fridge for up to 5 days.

CONTINUED ➤

NOTES:

I highly recommend using organic ginger, which has a more intense flavor than non-organic ginger.

Feel free to use as little or as much maple syrup and lime juice as you like. These measurements are just my preference.

If you don't have a nut milk bag, simply line a fine-mesh strainer with three layers of cheesecloth and place it over the bowl. Pour the ginger juice through it. Gather the four corners of each of the cheesecloths, twist them all together, and squeeze the ginger mixture to extract the juice.

Want an extra kick? Stir some cayenne pepper into the juice along with the maple syrup and lime juice.

Not-So-Traditional Green Smoothie

(GLUTEN-FREE)

MAKES: 1 SMOOTHIE
PREPARATION: 5 MINUTES

○ ○

1 cup cold unsweetened soy milk

1 banana, frozen and sliced

1 packed cup (1½ oz/50 g) spinach

1½ heaping tbsp toasted salted
   pistachios, plus more chopped
   for garnish

1 tbsp chia seeds

1 tbsp hemp hearts

1 pitted date

○

JUST WHEN YOU THOUGHT you had tried all the variations of green smoothies, here comes roasted pistachio! Yes, I know, pistachios are a bit of a fancy addition to a (by now) rather traditional morning drink, but if you are like me and, having tried countless smoothie recipes, are looking for a way to add a little luxury to your green smoothie, this variation might just be what you are looking for. And if you're new to green smoothies, this sweet, creamy, nutty, slightly smoky, and satisfying breakfast smoothie might just change your preconceived ideas about green smoothies.

○ ○ ○

Blend all the ingredients in a high-speed blender on the highest power level until smooth. Transfer to your favorite glass, top with chopped pistachios, if desired, and enjoy.

NOTE:

Because you are using whole nuts, using a high-speed blender is a must to ensure that you end up with a silky smoothie.

Spicy Berry Protein Smoothie

(CUSTOMIZABLE) (GLUTEN-FREE)

MAKES: 1 SMOOTHIE
PREPARATION: 5 MINUTES

IN THE LAST few decades, smoothies have definitely carved out their own space in the food world. Although there are hundreds of recipes for smoothies, they are one of my favorite breakfasts to improvise and get creative with on weekdays. I love playing around with different fruits, mixing up the liquids (Ever made a smoothie with chilled chai? Delicious!), and incorporating various spices and even vegetables. This smoothie is a nourishing drink I came up with while brainstorming for a satiating breakfast packed with proteins to keep me full for a few hours. It features healthy fats from hemps hearts, chia seeds, and peanut butter, as well as lots of vitamins from fruits. My favorite creative twist: red chili for a little heat.

○ ○

5 oz (150 g) silken tofu, drained

1 cup cold water

1 scoop unsweetened, unflavored vegan protein powder (I like Garden of Life's Raw Organic Protein)

1 ripe banana (see note)

1 cup frozen berries (I like a mix of blueberries and strawberries)

2 tbsp hemp hearts

1 tbsp chia seeds

1 tbsp natural crunchy or smooth peanut butter

1 small red chili (see note)

1–2 Bam, Medjool, or Habibi dates, optional for extra sweetness

○ ○ ○

Blend all the ingredients in a high-speed blender until smooth. Enjoy immediately.

NOTES:

If you are using a frozen banana, you will need between 1/3 cup and 1 cup more liquid, depending on your desired consistency. You could opt for water or unsweetened plant-based milk.

If you are sensitive to heat, cut the chili in half or remove its seeds before blending.

You can easily add a handful of fresh spinach to get your greens, but beware, the color might not be the most appetizing.

Frozen Chocolate Coffee Smoothie

(GLUTEN-FREE) (EXTRA PREP)

MAKES: 1 SMOOTHIE
PREPARATION: 5 MINUTES
RESTING: 8 HOURS

THERE WAS A TIME when my husband and I handled the marketing and Canadian import for a fair-trade jewelry brand. This led to us attending multiple conventions and festivals to promote the brand and sell its items, including at the Wanderlust yoga festival in Mont-Tremblant, Quebec, where a small organic bistro sold the most amazing smoothies. One of them was a life-changing coffee-flavored smoothie. It was cold, sweet, chocolatey, *and* had caffeine—the perfect midafternoon treat when the sun was blazing and we needed a refreshment that could also give us a little boost of energy to end the day. This recipe is my version, which I love as a kick start to my spring and summer mornings. Bear in mind that this is not a throw-everything-in-a-blender-and-enjoy type of smoothie; it requires a bit of extra prep to freeze the soy milk into ice cubes. This extra care makes a world of difference, giving it a thick and creamy texture.

○ ○

1 cup strong coffee

⅔ cup original sweetened soy milk (see note)

1 ripe banana

1 tbsp nut or seed butter of choice (see note)

1 tbsp hemp hearts

1 tbsp Dutch-processed cocoa powder

⅛ tsp ground cinnamon

1–2 Bam, Medjool, or Habibi dates, optional for extra sweetness (see note)

Hemp hearts, for garnish, optional

○ ○ ○

The night before making the smoothie, prep the ingredients: Refrigerate the coffee. Pour the soy milk into ice cube molds and freeze overnight. Peel the banana and cut it into slices, then place in a single layer in a container and freeze overnight.

The next day, in a blender, blend all the ingredients except the dates on high speed until smooth. Taste and add 1 to 2 dates if you want a sweeter smoothie. Top with hemp hearts, if desired, and enjoy immediately.

NOTES:

Original soy milk contains sugar, which I find works best for this recipe. If you use an unsweetened soy milk, make sure to add at least 1 date to your drink.

I find that the best nut butter for this smoothie is almond butter, but because I have an intolerance to it, I opt for peanut butter whenever I make it.

Lavender London Fog

(GLUTEN-FREE) (NUT/SEED-FREE)

MAKES: 1 SERVING
PREPARATION: 1 MINUTE
COOKING: 5 MINUTES

I AM A coffee person through and through. However, having grown up with a Russian mom, tea has always had a big place in my family life. Even back in Congo, we would often enjoy a cup of tea—made from fragrant, locally grown lemongrass—at night. After we moved to Canada, we continued this tradition, enjoying a cup with dessert nightly. My mom introduced our family to a whole new variety of teas, and when it came to Earl Grey, my mind was blown! I fell in love with its strong floral flavor and lovely notes of bergamot. Make my version when you want to slow down and treat yourself on a gray day: the lavender and maple syrup are the little touches of luxury that highlight even more the floral flavor profile. Enjoy in your favorite cup.

1 cup water

1 tbsp loose-leaf Earl Grey tea

½ tsp food-grade lavender buds

½ cup unsweetened soy milk

1 tsp maple syrup, plus more to taste

In a small pot, bring the water, Earl Grey, and lavender buds to a boil over high heat.

Add the soy milk and maple syrup. Reduce the heat to low and simmer for 3 minutes. Taste and add more maple syrup to your liking (the sweet spot for me is 2 teaspoons).

Pour the tea through a sieve into your favorite cup and enjoy.

Whenever my mom hosts family dinners, she pours her heart into the preparation, spending hours in the kitchen carefully putting together dishes that will complement each other and that she knows we adore. For those gatherings, rather than creating a large main dish, she tends to opt for a variety of side dishes. From her baked mushrooms to her creamy avocado salad to her herby pampushki, shuba, and much more, I have always been in awe of how my mom gives so much time and attention to making even the smallest of dishes.

In this chapter, I want to build upon my mom's approach in the kitchen by encouraging you to be present, taking your time with each ingredient and every step regardless of how quick or simple the recipe is.

The dishes featured in the pages that follow are veggie-forward and can be enjoyed on their own as a snack or light meal but are also great paired with other side dishes.

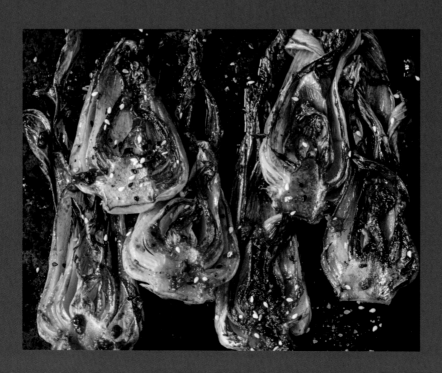

Small Plates
and Salads

Mini Blinis with Smoked Tomato

(NUT/SEED-FREE) (EXTRA PREP)

MAKES: 24–26 MINI BLINIS
PREPARATION: 30 MINUTES
COOKING: 30 MINUTES
RESTING: 8 HOURS

MINI BLINIS (*blinis* is Russian for *crepes*) have been one of my mom's traditional Christmas dishes for decades. Usually topped with smoked salmon, a dollop of sour cream, and capers, this dish is synonymous with celebrations. My veganized version features a star ingredient: marinated Roma tomatoes as the "smoked salmon." Preparing them requires you to employ a few fun techniques: blanching, coring, and marinating the tomatoes overnight in a mixture of tamari, liquid smoke, and seaweed. These are then served on pillowy mini blinis, along with silky vegan cream cheese, salty capers, and herbaceous dill. All the flavors build on each other to create the perfect little appetizer or amuse-bouche that is sure to be a crowd-pleaser!

SMOKED TOMATO

1 tbsp + 1½ tsp water

1 tbsp + ½ tsp tamari

1½ tsp olive oil

¼ tsp liquid smoke (see note)

¼ tsp ground seaweed (see note)

2 firm Roma tomatoes

MINI BLINIS

¾ cup (105 g) all-purpose flour

1½ tsp baking powder

½ tsp organic cane sugar

¼ tsp sea salt

¾ cup (185 ml) unsweetened soy milk

1 tsp avocado oil

Melted vegan butter or margarine, for cooking

PREPARE THE SMOKED TOMATO

Place the water, tamari, olive oil, liquid smoke, and seaweed in a glass container with a lid. Set aside.

Fill a saucepan with water and bring it to a boil.

Meanwhile, make 4 long and shallow lengthwise incisions in each tomato, from end to end. Place the tomatoes in the boiling water and cook for 1 minute. Drain the tomatoes, then run them under cold water for 2 minutes.

Remove the tomatoes' skins (it should come off easily after blanching) and quarter the tomatoes lengthwise. Scoop out the core and the seeds (freeze these to use in sauces).

Cut each tomato quarter into 4 to 6 pieces, depending on the size of tomatoes, and add to the tamari mixture. Put the lid on the container, then shake it a few times to fully coat the tomatoes with the marinade. Place in the fridge to marinate overnight.

CONTINUED ➤

Vegan cream cheese or vegan
  sour cream

Capers

Fresh dill

Freshly cracked black pepper

PREPARE THE BLINIS

In a small bowl, stir together the flour, baking powder, sugar, and salt. Add the soy milk and avocado oil and stir until well combined.

Heat a medium or large pan over medium heat. Using a silicone brush, brush the entire surface of the pan with melted butter.

Scoop the blini batter into the pan, using 1 heaping teaspoon of batter per blini, spreading the batter slightly into a circle using your spoon. Fit in as many blinis as you can while still leaving space between them to facilitate their flipping. Cook for 1 to 2 minutes, until golden. Flip and cook for another minute.

Repeat until you have used all the batter. If the pan gets too hot and starts to smoke, reduce the heat to medium-low.

Let the mini blinis cool completely before serving.

ASSEMBLE THE BLINIS

Dollop some vegan cream cheese onto the mini blinis. Top with 1 or 2 slices of smoked tomato, 1 or 2 capers, fresh dill, and a crack of pepper. Enjoy after assembly. Alternatively, store all the elements separately in the fridge for up to 3 days. You can eat your mini blinis cold or warm by microwaving them on medium power for 15 to 30 seconds.

NOTES:

Liquid smoke is a natural byproduct of burning wood that gives food a smoky flavor. It's found in most grocery stores in the sauces aisle, but if you can't find any, you can substitute ½ teaspoon of smoked paprika.

If you don't have ground seaweed, simply blend up a nori sheet and use ¼ teaspoon of the powder.

Shuba

(GLUTEN-FREE) (NUT/SEED-FREE)
(EXTRA PREP)

MAKES: 6 SERVINGS
PREPARATION: 30 MINUTES
COOKING: 30 MINUTES
RESTING: 3 HOURS

SHUBA IS A TRADITIONAL Russian and Ukrainian salad consisting of layers of smoked herring and grated carrots, beets, and potatoes. These are all held together by a mayo-based dressing. When I was growing up, shuba conjured up the holidays for me, and thanks to my aunt, who found a way to veganize this family classic, I continue to enjoy this salad on special occasions. I love getting all the ingredients ready in anticipation of sharing this salad with loved ones—and having a slice of it myself. From boiling and grating the vegetables to preparing the dressing, soaking the seaweed in tamari (to replace the traditional herring), and carefully layering all the flavors, when making this salad I'm reminded to slow down and enjoy the process. I know it will be tempting to enjoy this salad right away after all the love you put into it, but I recommend chilling it for at least 2 hours (and up to overnight) to let the flavors develop.

SHUBA

2 Yukon Gold potatoes, unpeeled

2 beets, unpeeled

1 large carrot, unpeeled

1 bay leaf

1 tsp sea salt, plus more for salad assembly

¼ tsp black pepper, plus more to taste

½ tsp garlic powder

1 small onion, finely diced

1½ tsp lemon juice

DRESSING

3 tbsp Homemade Mayo (p. 258) or store-bought vegan mayonnaise

1 tbsp water

Place the potatoes, beets, carrot, bay leaf, salt, and pepper in a large pot. Cover with water, put the lid on, and bring to a boil over high heat.

Reduce the heat to medium and cook, covered, until all the vegetables are fork-tender. Remove each as they finish cooking, transferring them to a bowl. The potatoes should be ready first, followed by the carrot, and finally the beets.

Place the bowl of veggies in the fridge to cool them completely, about 1 to 2 hours.

Once the veggies are completely cooled, peel and grate the potatoes into their own bowl, then do the same for the carrots and then the beets (I recommend doing it in this order to prevent the color of the beets from transferring from your hands onto the other vegetables).

To the bowl with the grated potatoes, add the garlic powder, a pinch of salt, and a pinch of pepper. Mix and set aside.

In a separate bowl, mix together the diced onion and lemon juice. Set aside.

CONTINUED ➤

3 sheets of nori, torn or cut in
¼-inch pieces

3 tbsp tamari

GARNISH (OPTIONAL)

Finely chopped chives or fresh
parsley

For the dressing, in a small bowl, mix together the mayo and water until smooth. Set aside.

For the tamari seaweed, in a separate bowl, mix the nori with the tamari until the nori has absorbed all the liquid. Set aside.

Remove the bottom of an 8-inch springform pan and place the ring on your serving plate (see note). Evenly spread the seaweed in the springform pan. Sprinkle evenly with the onion mixture, then with half of the potato mixture.

Drizzle 2 teaspoons of dressing over the potatoes, then spread it out using the back of a spoon or a silicone spatula. Top with the remaining potato mixture. Drizzle on 2 teaspoons of dressing, then spread it out evenly.

Top with the grated carrots, spread in an even layer. Cover with half of the grated beets. Top the beets with 2 teaspoons of dressing, spreading it to cover the beets. Top with the remaining beets. Drizzle the remaining mayo mixture over the beets, then spread evenly.

Cover the springform pan with foil or a plate and refrigerate for at least 2 hours before garnishing with a sprinkling of finely chopped chives. Store in the fridge, tightly covered with foil, for up to 3 days.

NOTES:

If you don't have a springform pan, form the layers directly on a plate. I recommend using a 9-inch plate to help keep the size of the shuba to about 8 inches in diameter.

Layering cheat sheet:

- *Tamari seaweed*
- *All the onion mixture*
- *Half of the potato mixture*
- *2 teaspoons of dressing*
- *Remaining potato mixture*
- *2 teaspoons of dressing*
- *All the carrots*
- *Half of the beets*
- *2 teaspoons of dressing*
- *Remaining beets*
- *Remaining dressing*

Watermelon "Tuna"

(GLUTEN-FREE) (NUT/SEED-FREE)
(EXTRA PREP)

MAKES: 1 CUP
PREPARATION: 10 MINUTES
COOKING: 2 HOURS 10 MINUTES
RESTING: 5 HOURS

○

IF YOU'RE NOT VEGAN, you might be thinking, "First 'smoked salmon' made out of tomatoes, in her mini blinis recipe, now 'tuna' made with watermelon. Vegans these days!" I won't try to convince you that this recipe offers a perfect replacement for tuna. However, for the longest time, I didn't think there could be any vegan alternative for raw fish—until I learned about baking watermelon. If you're like me and love to experiment in the kitchen, discovering new ways to prepare ingredients, then you might have fun making this recipe. Baking the watermelon allows a lot of its water to evaporate, and helps it to soak up the flavor of the marinade, changing the texture completely so it's closer to that of raw fish. It is delicious straight out of the oven, tossed in spicy mayo, on its own or on avocado toast, or in poke bowls or homemade sushi rolls. It's also a key ingredient in my Avocado, Mango, and Watermelon "Tuna" Salad with Sesame Dressing (p. 94), just make sure to skip the coating in spicy mayo.

○ ○

¼ cup tamari

¼ cup rice vinegar

2 tsp sesame oil

1 tsp ground seaweed (see note on page 84)

4½ cups (25 oz/700 g) cubed seedless watermelon flesh (½-inch cubes)

SPICY MAYO

2 tbsp Homemade Mayo (p. 258) or store-bought vegan mayonnaise

2 tsp sambal oelek or sriracha, or more to taste

○ ○ ○

In a large glass container with a lid, whisk together the tamari, rice vinegar, sesame oil, and ground seaweed. Add the cubed watermelon, seal the container, and shake it gently to distribute the marinade. Refrigerate for 2 hours.

Preheat the oven to 250°F. Line a baking sheet with parchment paper large enough to cover the entire baking sheet and its sides.

Using a slotted spoon, place the watermelon on the parchment paper.

Bake for 2 hours, flipping the watermelon cubes halfway through the cooking time. Increase the oven temperature to 350°F and bake for 8 to 10 more minutes, until the cubes are slightly charred.

Transfer immediately to a clean glass airtight container, seal, and refrigerate until cold, about 3 hours.

If using for my Avocado, Mango, and Tuna Salad, skip this step. Right before serving, mix together the mayo and sambal oelek in a small bowl. Add the spicy mayo to the chilled watermelon, tossing to coat.

Best served fresh. Store in the fridge in an airtight container for up to 3 days.

Herby Baked Mushrooms

(GLUTEN-FREE) (NUT/SEED-FREE)

MAKES: 4 SERVINGS
PREPARATION: 5 MINUTES
COOKING: 20 MINUTES

○ ○

1 lb (454 g) button mushrooms
  (see note)

2½ tbsp tamari

4 garlic cloves, finely minced

1 tsp olive oil

1 tsp dried parsley

1 tsp dried basil

½ tsp sweet paprika

¼ tsp black pepper

⅓ packed cup fresh parsley,
  chopped (see note)

○

MUSHROOMS PLAY a rather big part in Russian cuisine and in my family's culinary traditions. My mom likes to sauté them with onions and stuff traditional varenyky (p. 189) and even puff pastry with them. She also often pickles them with other ingredients like celeriac. However, I have to admit, I enjoy her baked mushrooms the best. What I love about this recipe is that it is a one-pan dish and it is very forgiving. It's also the type of dish that becomes better with time. Don't get me wrong, the mushrooms are still finger-lickin' good straight out of the oven, but if you let them cool off a little bit, the heat from the mushrooms will help release even more flavor from the parsley, adding more depth to the dish.

○ ○ ○

Preheat the oven to 400°F.

Place the mushrooms in a 9-inch pie or square baking dish. Top with all the ingredients except the parsley and toss to coat.

Bake for 10 minutes, then give the mushrooms a stir. Bake for another 10 minutes.

Remove from the oven, sprinkle in the parsley, and stir to distribute evenly.

Serve hot, warm, or even chilled. Store in the fridge in an airtight container for up to 3 days.

NOTES:

If your button mushrooms are chunky, just cut them in half.

Replace the parsley with coriander, if desired.

Olivier Salad

(GLUTEN-FREE) (NUT/SEED-FREE)

(EXTRA PREP)

MAKES: 4 SERVINGS
PREPARATION: 20 MINUTES
COOKING: 20 MINUTES
RESTING: 2 HOURS

OLIVER SALAD—A QUINTESSENTIAL Russian salad. Although there are multiple variations of this Eastern European classic, it's generally made of diced potatoes, carrots, hard-boiled eggs, pickles, ham, and canned peas, all tossed in a creamy mayo-based dressing. Of all the recipes in this cookbook, this is the one I owe almost entirely to my mom, who veganized it. Similar to the recipe for shuba (p. 85), the prep for this recipe is somewhat methodical: the potatoes and carrots need to be boiled, cooled, and cut into small cubes before being tossed in a bright dressing. The apple adds sweetness, while the green peas add a beautiful pop of color. Make it up to 1 day in advance and bring to a celebratory gathering as a fun twist to the usual potato salad.

2 Yukon Gold or russet potatoes, unpeeled

1 carrot, unpeeled

1 bay leaf

½ tsp sea salt

½ tsp pepper

½ cup frozen green peas

½ Gala or Pink Lady apple, cored

1 large dill pickle, diced

2 tbsp capers, coarsely chopped

2 tbsp finely sliced chives or green onions

DRESSING

3 tbsp Homemade Mayo (p. 258) or store-bought vegan mayonnaise

2 tbsp lemon juice

1 tbsp pickle juice

½ tsp maple syrup

¼ tsp garlic powder

¼ tsp sea salt

¼ tsp black pepper

Place the potatoes, carrot, bay leaf, salt, and pepper in a pot set over high heat. Cover with water and bring to a boil.

Reduce the heat to medium and cook, partly covered, until the potatoes and carrot are fork-tender, about 20 minutes.

Drain then transfer the vegetables to a bowl and let cool completely. You can accelerate the cooling process by placing them in the fridge for 1 to 2 hours.

Put the frozen peas in a small bowl and cover with boiling water. Let sit for 2 minutes, then drain and rinse with cold water. Transfer to a salad bowl.

Peel the cooled potatoes and carrot, and the apple, then dice into ⅓-inch cubes. Add to the bowl with the peas, along with the pickle, capers, and chives.

Prepare the dressing in a separate bowl by whisking together all the ingredients until smooth. Pour over the salad, tossing to coat. Enjoy immediately or chill for later consumption—I find this salad is best enjoyed after it's chilled for 1 to 2 hours in the fridge. Store in the fridge in an airtight container for up to 3 days.

Avocado, Mango, and Watermelon "Tuna" Salad with Sesame Dressing

(GLUTEN-FREE) (NUT/SEED-FREE)
(EXTRA PREP)

MAKES: 4 SERVINGS
PREPARATION: 10 MINUTES

○

THIS BRIGHT AND FRESH salad bursts with flavors and truly feels like a tropical dish you might eat when away on vacation. It is luxurious, rich, sweet, salty, and delightfully tangy. It features my Watermelon "Tuna" (p. 89), which you'll need to prepare in advance. As you slowly bring all the ingredients together, taste along the way and notice how each flavor complements the others. The cooked watermelon brings sweetness, umami, and a lovely texture to the entire dish. The avocado brings richness, while the mangoes add sweetness and tanginess. Serve this salad as a side to lighten up a meal, or scoop it into lettuce leaves and enjoy it with Lemon Pepper Tempeh (p. 172) for a flavor-packed lunch!

○○

DRESSING

2 tbsp lime juice, plus more to taste

1 tsp sesame oil

¼ tsp sea salt, plus more to taste

¼ tsp garlic powder

1 or 2 pinches of cayenne pepper, optional

SALAD

½ batch of Watermelon "Tuna" (p. 89), without the Spicy Mayo

2 avocadoes, cut in ½-inch cubes (see note)

1 Ataulfo mango, peeled, pitted, and cut in ¼-inch cubes (see note)

¼ cup finely diced red onion

¼ cup loosely packed fresh coriander, coarsely chopped

Black and white sesame seeds, for garnish, optional

○○○

For the dressing, in a small bowl, whisk together all the ingredients. Set aside.

To assemble the salad, use a slotted spoon to place the Watermelon "Tuna" in a serving bowl, leaving behind as much of its juices as possible. Add the avocadoes, mango, red onion, and coriander.

Pour the dressing over the salad, tossing to coat well. Taste and add more lime juice, salt, or cayenne to your liking.

Garnish with sesame seeds and enjoy.

NOTES:

This salad is best enjoyed cold. So, depending on your schedule, either chill your avocados and mango for at least 1 hour before preparing the salad or use room-temperature avocados and mango, then chill the salad in the fridge for at least 1 hour before serving.

If you cannot find an atulfo mango, you can use the more traditional Tommy Atkins mango, but choose one that is not too ripe and use only half to three-quarters of it in this recipe.

Massaged Kale Salad

(CUSTOMIZABLE) (GLUTEN-FREE)

(NUT/SEED-FREE OPTION)

(EXTRA PREP)

MAKES: 4 SERVINGS
PREPARATION: 10 MINUTES

CREATING THIS RECIPE required a few trial runs. I knew I wanted to create a salad that features my rich, umami-packed Tamari, Balsamic Vinegar, and Nutritional Yeast Sauce (p. 261). After trying that sauce on salads with greens like spinach and arugula, I decided that it needed a heartier carrier. I used to have a real aversion to kale. I would add it to my smoothies, and tried using it in salads, and every time I was disappointed. Then I discovered that if you take the time to massage the kale with dressing for a few minutes to soften it up, it turns into a glorious, magical cruciferous vegetable! So, I came to settle on using kale for this salad, since its slight bitterness beautifully complements the sauce. The pomegranate arils (aka little gems from the gods) add a burst of sweetness to this salad, and the onion and carrot bring a lovely texture.

4 packed cups curly kale, stems removed, cut in bite-sized pieces

¼ cup Tamari, Balsamic Vinegar, and Nutritional Yeast Sauce (p. 261), plus more to taste

1 small carrot, peeled and grated (see note)

⅓ cup pomegranate arils (see note)

¼ cup diced red onion

2 tbsp hemp hearts (see note)

Black pepper, to taste

Place the kale leaves in a salad bowl and drizzle with the Tamari, Balsamic Vinegar, and Nutritional Yeast Sauce. Massage the kale with clean hands for 3 minutes or until the leaves have shrunk in size and softened.

Sprinkle the grated carrot, pomegranate arils, red onion, and hemp hearts over the kale.

Give the salad a toss. Taste and add more dressing, to your liking, and a touch of pepper for an extra kick. Enjoy after assembly or store in the fridge for up to 24 hours.

NOTES:

You can play around with the vegetables in this salad by replacing the carrot with raw shredded beets or finely diced bell peppers. Pomegranate arils can be swapped with dried fruits such as raisins or cranberries.

Replace the hemp hearts with roasted sunflower seeds, pepitas, or chopped smoked almonds. If you are allergic or intolerant to seeds, simply omit the hemp hearts.

Creamy Avocado Salad

(GLUTEN-FREE) (NUT/SEED-FREE)

MAKES: 4 SERVINGS
PREPARATION: 10 MINUTES

○ ○

½ red onion, thinly sliced

½ tsp sea salt, plus more to taste

2 avocadoes, cut in ½-inch cubes
(see note)

1 tomato, cut in ½-inch cubes
(see note)

DRESSING

1 tbsp Homemade Mayo (p. 258) or
store-bought vegan mayonnaise

2 tbsp lemon juice

1 garlic clove, grated using a
Microplane

¼ tsp black pepper

○

ONE OF MY most distinct food memories of my arrival in Canada in 2002 is of my mom making this avocado salad for us. This was *way* before the avocado rose to fame, and before it made its way onto toasts all around the world. I remember eight-year-old me looking at my mom in awe as she carefully scrunched the onions with salt to soften them and then tossed all the ingredients together in the beautiful glass bowl she had found at a Montreal thrift shop. Whenever I had a bite of this salad as a child, I felt the love of my mom—and that still holds true today. I always thought this salad was complicated to make and required fancy ingredients, but it truly doesn't. It does, however, require you to embrace getting your hands a little dirty (only with onion and salt, though!).

○ ○ ○

Place the red onion in a serving bowl and sprinkle it with salt. Using your hands, squeeze and gently massage the onion slices for about 30 seconds, until softened.

Add the cubed avocadoes and tomatoes.

For the dressing, in a small bowl, whisk together the mayo, lemon juice, grated garlic, and pepper. Set aside.

Pour the dressing over the salad, tossing to coat well. Taste and add more salt to your liking. Enjoy.

NOTES:

This salad is best enjoyed cold. So, depending on your schedule, either chill your avocados for at least 1 hour before preparing the salad or use room-temperature avocados, then chill the salad in the fridge for at least 1 hour before serving.

If you only have cherry tomatoes on hand (or don't feel like cubing tomatoes), you can swap the cubed tomato with 1 cup of halved cherry tomatoes.

Coconut Rice

(GLUTEN-FREE) (NUT/SEED-FREE)

MAKES: 4 SERVINGS
PREPARATION: 5 MINUTES
COOKING: 15 MINUTES
RESTING: 10 MINUTES

○

FUNNILY, THE FIRST TIME I was left in charge of cooking for my brothers while my mom visited her parents in Ukraine, one of the things I was most stressed about was making rice. My mom's has always been absolutely perfect—soft and fluffy, with perfectly separated grains. Expectations were high. My mom was amused by my stress, but also encouraged me to simply follow her clearly laid-out steps and to trust the process—this last part has always been one of her keys to culinary success. So, with her expert tips and after a few (slightly stressful but successful) attempts, I can now proudly say rice no longer intimidates me—I've even gotten pretty creative with this otherwise straightforward dish, which is how coconut rice came to be. Light, coconutty, and fragrant, this side dish is a staple in my home and one I love to enjoy alongside just about any main, including Saka Saka (p. 133) and Peanut Butter and Sweet Potato Stew (p. 141).

○ ○

1 cup white basmati rice

1 cup water

1 cup full-fat coconut milk, from a can (see note)

½ tsp sea salt

Toasted unsweetened shredded coconut, optional

○ ○ ○

Rinse the rice in a fine-mesh strainer under cold water, shifting it with your fingers, until the water runs completely clear.

Transfer to a saucepan and add the water, coconut milk, and salt. Give it all a stir, cover, and bring to a boil over high heat.

Reduce the heat to low and remove the lid for a minute or so, to prevent the liquid from boiling over (it will be bubbling up at this point). Then put the lid back on and cook the mixture for 12 minutes or until all the liquid has been absorbed.

Remove the pot from the heat and let sit, covered, for 10 minutes.

Fluff up the rice with a fork and serve, garnished with toasted shredded coconut, if desired. This rice is best eaten fresh, but you can also store it in the fridge in an airtight container for up to 2 days.

NOTE:

For a lighter version of this rice, opt for light coconut milk instead of the full-fat version.

NOTES:

When choosing the perfect plantains to fry, avoid any that are green and hard to the touch, or any that are fully yellow. Instead, opt for ones with lots of dark spots, and even with black areas on the skins. They should also be slightly soft to the touch.

Add a little kick: before flipping the plantains, sprinkle them with chili powder and/or cayenne pepper. Or, for a smoky flavor, season with a touch of smoked paprika before flipping in the pan.

Pan-Fried Plantains

(CUSTOMIZABLE) (GLUTEN-FREE)
(NUT/SEED-FREE OPTION)

MAKES: 4 SERVINGS
PREPARATION: 2 MINUTES
COOKING: 10 MINUTES

FRIED PLANTAINS ARE what I like to call *golden delicacies*. Soft and deliciously sweet, they are one of the easiest side dishes (and snacks!) that can be prepped and ready in under 15 minutes. When frying them, you will have to be entirely present, as they can quickly go from golden brown to very dark, but when prepared right, they'll add a wonderful sweetness to a savory meal. This recipe is just the base recipe, so if you are feeling extra fancy, play with adding your favorite spices. The possibilities are endless! Enjoy these golden delicacies alongside Coconut Rice (p. 100), Fufu (p. 118), and Saka Saka (p. 133) for my ultimate Congolese-inspired feast.

∘ ∘

2 ripe plantains

Neutral cooking oil (such as avocado, canola, or melted refined coconut)

Sea salt

Black pepper

Seasonings of choice, optional (see note)

∘ ∘ ∘

Cut a ½ inch off each end of the plantain. Peel the plantains by running a sharp knife through each ridge of the peel, from one end of the plantain to the other, making sure the knife does not go much deeper than the skin. Peel off the skin and discard. Cut the plantains into ½-inch slices and set aside.

Preheat the oven to 200°F. Line a plate with paper towel and place it in the oven.

Heat a large heavy-bottomed pan (such as a cast-iron skillet) over medium heat. Add enough oil to generously cover the entire surface of the pan and heat for 2 to 3 minutes. Sprinkle a few drops of water into the pan; if the oil sizzles, the oil is hot enough for the plantain slices. If it does not sizzle, wait a few more seconds, then test it again.

Gently drop a few slices of plantain into the pan, being careful not to splatter the hot oil or overcrowd the pan.

If adding seasonings other than salt and pepper (see note), sprinkle them on the plantains. Cook the plantains for 2 to 3 minutes, until browned. Flip and cook for another minute or so.

Transfer the fried plantains to the prepared plate in the oven to keep warm. Repeat the process with the remaining plantain slices.

Season with salt and pepper to your liking. Keep warm in the oven until ready to serve.

The Ultimate Mashed Potatoes

(GLUTEN-FREE) (NUT/SEED-FREE)

MAKES: 4 SERVINGS
PREPARATION: 10 MINUTES
COOKING: 15 MINUTES

WHEN I WAS A KID, my mom made mashed potatoes at least once a week and, every time, they were a real treat. At some point, we replaced them with grains, so it's only in the last few years that I reconnected with my love of mashed potatoes. They are honestly one of the most satisfying side dish, in my eyes. Soft, pillowy, rich, and slightly cheesy, my mashed potatoes can be prepared any day of the week. Although made with a humble root vegetable, they always add a little pillowy luxury to the meal. I love the process of folding fresh chives and garlic powder into mashed potatoes, as both ingredients add flavor and give them an extra oomph. But if you are looking for a more traditional mashed potato recipe, feel free to skip both of those additions.

4 Yukon Gold potatoes, peeled and cubed

2 garlic cloves, peeled and coarsely chopped

½ tsp sea salt, plus more to taste

⅛ tsp baking powder

3 tbsp unsalted vegan butter, plus more to taste

⅓ cup unsweetened soy milk, plus more to taste

2 tbsp nutritional yeast

2 tbsp chopped chives, optional

½ tsp garlic powder, optional

Place the potatoes, garlic, and salt in a large pot. Cover with water and a lid and bring to a boil over high heat.

Reduce the heat to medium and cook, covered (or partially covered if necessary to prevent the water from boiling over), until the potatoes are very soft, 12 to 15 minutes.

Drain, then return the potatoes and garlic to the pot. Sprinkle with the baking powder. Add the butter, then mash, using a potato masher, to combine and achieve your desired level of smoothness.

Add the soy milk, nutritional yeast, chives, and garlic powder, if using. Stir together, then taste and adjust the salt level to your liking. Add more soy milk or butter for extra richness, if desired.

Enjoy as a side to any meal. Store in the fridge in an airtight container for up to 3 days.

Garlicky Roasted Potatoes

(CUSTOMIZABLE) (GLUTEN-FREE)
(NUT/SEED-FREE)

MAKES: 4 SERVINGS
PREPARATION: 10 MINUTES
COOKING: 1 HOUR

○ ○

4 russet potatoes, unpeeled
   and cut in ½-inch cubes

1 tsp baking soda

1 tsp sea salt, divided

2 garlic cloves, grated using
   a Microplane

2 tbsp nutritional yeast

2 tbsp avocado oil

2 tsp dried onion

1 tsp garlic powder

½ tsp black pepper

○

EVERY COOKBOOK I have ever owned includes a version of roasted potatoes, so I knew I too had to share my go-to recipe. After playing around with countless ways to make roasted potatoes, I found that adding one extra step to the preparation turned this humble vegetable into an even bigger star. The key is boiling the russet potatoes—yes, *russet* potatoes are a must, as their starch makes them extra crispy when baked—before roasting them. This way, they are precooked when they hit the baking sheet, which results in potatoes that are soft on the inside and crispy on the outside, *every time*! These potatoes are coated in a mixture of nutritional yeast, dried onion, freshly grated garlic, *and* garlic powder, which together pack a punch. If you are a garlic lover, this one is definitely for you!

○ ○ ○

Place the potatoes, baking soda, and ½ teaspoon of salt in a saucepan. Cover with water and the lid and bring to a boil over high heat.

Once boiling, reduce the heat to medium and cook until the potatoes are fork-tender, 10 to 12 minutes.

Preheat the oven to 425°F. Line a baking sheet with parchment paper or a silicone mat.

Drain the potatoes, then return them to the pan along with the remaining ingredients (including the remaining ½ teaspoon of salt). Toss everything together using a silicone spatula.

Spread the potatoes evenly on the prepared baking sheet.

Bake for 20 minutes, then give the potatoes a toss and bake for another 15 to 20 minutes, until they are golden and crispy at the edges.

Enjoy with your favorite sauces or alongside my Tangy Aioli (p. 259).

NOTE:

This recipe is highly customizable. I love adding fresh herbs to this recipe—rosemary is my absolute favorite! Feel free to use your favorite herbs—just make sure to chop them finely.

Roasted Cauliflower with Caper-Raisin Sauce

(GLUTEN-FREE) (NUT/SEED-FREE)

MAKES: 4 SERVINGS
PREPARATION: 5 MINUTES
COOKING: 30 MINUTES

WHEN WE IMMIGRATED to Canada, my mom became in charge of cooking for the family and was always very interested in experimenting with new foods. For instance, it was only after we arrived here that she made cauliflower—a magic vegetable!—a classic in our household. This was long before it exploded in popularity and became the star ingredient in pizza crusts, stews, smoothies, and so much more. I think cauliflower definitely deserves its fame—it's such a versatile and tasty vegetable. In this recipe, the florets are simply seasoned and roasted on high heat until beautifully browned. I believe that flavor develops with color, so be sure not to rush the roasting process. Your patience will be rewarded when you serve your florets with the epic Caper-Raisin Sauce, which is the perfect mixture of sweet, salty, and tangy.

CAULIFLOWER

1 large cauliflower head, cut in bite-sized florets

2 tbsp olive oil

Sea salt, to taste

Black pepper, to taste

CAPER-RAISIN SAUCE

⅓ cup golden raisins

½ tsp lemon zest

2 tbsp lemon juice

1 tbsp capers

2 tsp olive oil

PREPARE THE CAULIFLOWER

Preheat the oven to 400°F. Line a baking sheet with foil and grease it with cooking spray or brush it with a neutral cooking oil (such as avocado, canola, or melted refined coconut). Alternatively, you can roast the cauliflower directly on the baking sheet, just make sure to oil the baking sheet.

Spread the cauliflower florets on the baking sheet, drizzle with the olive oil, and season generously with salt and pepper. Bake for 25 to 30 minutes, until fork-tender and browned, tossing the cauliflower at the 20-minute mark. Transfer to a serving bowl.

PREPARE THE SAUCE

While the cauliflower is baking, place the raisins in a small saucepan, cover with water, and bring to a boil over medium-high heat. Cook for 3 minutes or until the raisins are soft to the touch and rehydrated.

Drain and transfer to an immersion blender cup with the remaining sauce ingredients. Blend until the raisins are broken down into smaller pieces. The sauce should be relatively chunky. Alternatively, you can use a mini food processor or a blender with a small cup.

Spoon the sauce over the roasted cauliflower and enjoy. Store any leftovers separated in the fridge in airtight containers for up to 2 days.

Ricotta and Spinach Phyllo Cups

(CUSTOMIZABLE)　(NUT/SEED-FREE)
(EXTRA PREP)

MAKES: 8 CUPS
PREPARATION: 20 MINUTES
COOKING: 35 MINUTES
RESTING: 30 MINUTES

FLAKY AND BUTTERY on the outside, soft, fragrant, and savory on the inside, these phyllo cups were, once upon a time, one of my family's favorite weekend and special-occasion treats. As you make this recipe, I encourage you to really slow down and embrace the process of bringing all the elements together. Carefully follow the steps of cooking the ricotta, softening the onions, and caramelizing the mushrooms. And have fun buttering the phyllo sheets—I love thinking of the delicious crunch and richness this step will result in! Get creative and switch up the button mushrooms with your favorite type (oyster mushrooms are delicious); play with the spices or incorporate fresh herbs; fold in some sun-dried tomatoes or olives for an added layer of texture and flavor. The possibilities are truly endless! These are a crowd-pleaser, perfect as either a side dish or an appetizer.

2 tbsp olive oil

1 onion, diced

3 garlic cloves, minced

8 oz (227 g) button mushrooms, coarsely chopped

1½ tsp dried parsley

½ tsp sweet paprika

½ tsp sea salt, plus more to taste

⅛–¼ tsp chili flakes

Black pepper, to taste

1 packed cup (1½ oz/50 g) spinach or kale, coarsely chopped (see note)

1 batch of Nut-Free Ricotta (p. 264)

8 phyllo sheets, thawed

5 tbsp melted unsalted vegan butter, plus more for greasing

1 tbsp maple syrup

1 tbsp unsweetened soy milk

Heat a large pan over medium heat. Once hot, add the olive oil and onion and cook, stirring often with a wooden spoon, for 5 minutes or until the onion is translucent.

Stir in the garlic and mushrooms. Cook for 8 to 10 minutes, until the mushrooms are caramelized at the edges.

Sprinkle in the parsley, paprika, salt, chili flakes, and pepper. Stir and cook for another minute before adding the spinach. Cook until the spinach has wilted, then remove the pan from the heat and let the mixture cool for 15 minutes.

Transfer the mushroom mixture to a bowl. Stir in the ricotta. Taste and add more salt or pepper to your liking, then set aside while you prepare the phyllo cups.

Preheat the oven to 350°F. Lightly grease 8 cups of a muffin pan with melted butter or cooking spray.

CONTINUED ➤

Place a phyllo sheet on a clean work surface. Brush the phyllo sheet with the melted butter using a silicone brush—your phyllo sheet should not be soaked in butter; use about ¼ to ½ teaspoon of butter per layer. Fold the sheet in half lengthwise and brush again with butter. Fold the sheet in half lengthwise again and brush with butter. Fold the sheet in half lengthwise one last time. You should now have 8 layers of phyllo. Gently press the folded phyllo sheet into a muffin pan cup.

Repeat the process with the remaining 7 phyllo sheets.

Divide the mushroom-ricotta mixture among the phyllo cups. Gather the four corners of each phyllo cup and pinch them together to create a little bundle.

In a small bowl, mix together the maple syrup and soy milk. Lightly brush each phyllo bundle with the soy milk mixture.

Bake for 20 minutes or until golden. To add even more color to your cups, broil for 1 or 2 minutes at 500°F after baking.

Let cool for at least 15 minutes before enjoying. The cups are best eaten warm the same day; however, you can store them in an airtight container in the fridge for up to 3 days, reheating in the oven at 350°F for 5 minutes.

NOTE:

If using kale rather than spinach, be sure to remove the stems, and cut each leaf in pieces no bigger than 1 inch.

Pearl Barley Salad with Roasted Bell Peppers and Vegan Feta

(NUT/SEED-FREE) (EXTRA PREP)

MAKES: 4–6 SERVINGS
PREPARATION: 10 MINUTES
COOKING: 45 MINUTES
RESTING: 1 HOUR

I WILL BE 100% honest with you—the very green kind of salads are not one of my go-tos, and I rarely crave them, mostly because of the dozens of bad (and bland!) salad experiences I've had in restaurants. I am a much bigger fan of salads that feature many layers of flavors and textures. To make this salad come to life, you will have to spend a little extra time cooking the barley, to bring it to its chewy perfection, which will allow it to act as a perfect base for the other ingredients. The roasted bell peppers add a touch of smokiness and sweetness, and the brown lentils give this salad a nice bite while also making it a little more filling. The Kalamata olives and vegan feta add a kick of saltiness, while the parsley is the finishing touch of freshness that really ties this dish together.

1 cup pearl barley

3 cups water

½ tsp sea salt

1 tsp olive oil

½ cup dried brown lentils
  (see note)

1½ cups vegetable broth

1½ roasted red bell pepper, cut in
  ¼-inch pieces (see note)

½ cup pitted and coarsely chopped
  Kalamata olives or sun-dried
  tomatoes

½ cup crumbled vegan feta

⅓ packed cup fresh parsley,
  coarsely chopped

Rinse the barley, then place in a saucepan along with the water and salt. Cover and bring to a boil over high heat.

Reduce the heat to low and remove the lid. Continue cooking until the barley is tender and chewy, 12 to 15 minutes. Drain and transfer to a salad bowl. Drizzle with the olive oil, toss, and place in the fridge to cool.

Rinse the lentils, then place in a saucepan with the vegetable broth. Cover and bring to a boil over high heat.

Reduce the heat to medium-low and cook, covered, until tender but not mushy, 20 to 25 minutes.

Drain the lentils and transfer to the bowl with the barley. Refrigerate for 1 hour, giving the barley and lentils a toss every 15 minutes or so to accelerate the cooling process.

Prepare the dressing in a separate bowl by whisking together all the ingredients until smooth.

CONTINUED ➤

2 tbsp lemon juice

1 tbsp olive oil

1 tsp maple syrup

1 tsp Dijon mustard

¼ tsp garlic powder

¼ tsp sea salt

¼ tsp black pepper

To the salad bowl, add the bell peppers, olives, feta, and parsley.

Drizzle the dressing over the salad and give it all a toss. Enjoy after assembly or store in the fridge in an airtight container for up to 3 days.

NOTES:

You can replace the dried brown lentils with 1 cup of canned brown lentils, rinsed—no need to cook them in vegetable broth.

Use jarred roasted red bell peppers, or roast your own. To roast them, preheat the oven to 425°F and line a baking sheet with parchment paper or a silicone mat. Place 2 red bell peppers on the prepared baking sheet and bake for 40 minutes, flipping halfway through the cooking time. Remove from the oven, place in a bowl, and cover the bowl with a plate. Let the peppers steam for 20 minutes, then remove the core and skin and use 1½ bell peppers in this recipe. Use the remaining bell pepper in a sandwich or pasta sauce.

Stewed Greens

(GLUTEN-FREE) (NUT/SEED-FREE)

MAKES: 4–6 SERVINGS
PREPARATION: 5 MINUTES
COOKING: 10 MINUTES
RESTING: 10 MINUTES

THERE IS SOMETHING so satisfying about eating softened greens. However, one thing I struggled with when it came to cooking greens was how to stop them from turning a deep khaki color. Then my dad came along with his kitchen tricks and taught me that the key is to not cook the greens for more than 10 minutes, and to then immediately remove them from the heat and let them sit, covered, until fully cooked through. This has become a game changer! Now we can all enjoy delicious, juicy, melt-in-your-mouth greens that are vibrant in color and a great side to any meal. One tip: use a timer. Many of us are multitaskers in the kitchen, and it is easy to forget about a dish on the stovetop and, in the case of this recipe, that could mean overcooked greens.

10 loosely packed cups
   (10½ oz/300 g) fresh
   baby spinach

2 green onions, sliced

½ large green, orange, or
   yellow bell pepper, diced
   (see note)

½ onion, diced

½ cup water

2 tbsp canola oil

¾ tsp sea salt, plus more
   to taste

Black pepper, to taste

Place the spinach, green onions, bell pepper, onion, and water in a large saucepan, cover, and cook on high heat, stirring occasionally to help soften the spinach.

Once the spinach has shrunk to about half its original size, reduce the heat to low, add the canola oil, cover, and cook until the spinach is cooked through but still bright green.

Remove from the heat, season with salt and pepper, stir, cover, and let sit for 10 minutes to let the remaining veggies cook through.

Enjoy on its own, or alongside my Saucy White Kidney Beans (p. 148) and your grain of choice. Store leftovers in the fridge in an airtight container for up to 24 hours.

NOTE:

I find that green, orange, and yellow bell peppers look the prettiest against the vibrant green of the stewed spinach. However, you can use red bell pepper, if you like.

Fufu

(GLUTEN-FREE) (NUT/SEED-FREE)

MAKES: 4 SERVINGS
PREPARATION: 5 MINUTES
COOKING: 20 MINUTES
RESTING: 30 MINUTES

∘∘

2 cups (500 ml) water

2 cups (280 g) cassava flour
(see note)

FOR SERVING (OPTIONAL)
Saka Saka (p. 133), Peanut Butter
and Sweet Potato Stew (p. 141),
Saucy White Kidney Bans (p. 148),
and/or Stewed Greens (p. 117)

∘

FUFU IS A SIDE DISH that is very popular in many African countries, including in the Republic of Congo, where I was born. Although the ways to make it vary quite a bit from country to country and even from family to family, the version I ate most often as a child was made of only two ingredients: cassava flour and water. Both ingredients are cooked and stirred (constantly and vigorously!) until you get a thick, creamy paste that holds together. This recipe requires you to be attentive to both the texture and the flavor. If you don't cook the mixture long enough, you will end up with a bitter paste that does not hold together and is pretty much inedible, flavor-wise. If you get it right, you will end up with a thick, melt-in-your-mouth paste. It acts like bread does in many Western countries in that it is often eaten with soups or stews. The flavor of fufu is quite neutral, which makes it the perfect dipping agent.

∘∘∘

In a saucepan, whisk together the water and cassava flour until fully combined. Heat over medium heat, stirring often with a wooden spoon or a spatula.

Once the mixture starts to thicken, change color, and look slightly granulated and loose, while holding together relatively well (a little like polenta), reduce the heat to medium-low and stir constantly with a wooden spoon. The color of the mixture will go from almost white to light beige to a darker beige. One way to assess the readiness of the fufu is by tasting it as the mixture continues to cook. It will not be very tasty at first, and even halfway through cooking it will taste rather bitter and floury, but keep stirring, pushing the mixture to the sides of your saucepan.

Continue cooking and stirring until the fufu is thick, gummy, and has no floury, bitter taste. You can also pinch a bit of it with your fingertips; once it sticks together and holds its shape well, it is ready.

Let the fufu cool for 15 minutes in the pan. Cut 4 pieces of plastic wrap into 8-inch squares. Divide the fufu into four, then place each portion into the center of a square of plastic wrap. Gather and twist the corners of the plastic wrap together, forming the fufu into a ball.

Let the fufu cool for at least 15 minutes before unwrapping. Enjoy it alongside your chosen dish. Store leftovers in the fridge, covered with plastic wrap, for up to 2 days.

NOTE:

You can find cassava flour in most African grocery shops.

Pampushki

(NUT/SEED-FREE) (EXTRA PREP)

MAKES: 15 ROLLS
PREPARATION: 25 MINUTES
COOKING: 30 MINUTES
RESTING: 1 HOUR 15 MINUTES

AS MY MOM would say, these savory rolls are like a hug from a Ukrainian grandma: pillowy, soft, and comforting. The key to the success of these rolls is the dough. It's light and airy, and comes together with a few key ingredients, a little bit of love, and some oil. I have found that ensuring that the water is warm enough, letting the instant yeast bloom properly, and intentional kneading leads to the softest of doughs. The garlicky topping is the perfect finishing touch that takes these rolls to the next level. The result is doughy, garlicky, deliciously herbaceous rolls that your dinner guests won't be able to resist! Trust me, every time I serve these, they are gone in minutes.

○ ○

1 cup (250 ml) warm water
   (at about 120°F)

1 tbsp (15 g) organic cane sugar

½ tsp sea salt

1 (2¼ tsp/7 g) sachet instant yeast

3 tbsp + ¼ cup (105 ml) canola oil,
   divided, plus more for greasing

3 cups (420 g) all-purpose flour,
   divided

GARLICKY GLAZE

3 tbsp (45 ml) water

2 tbsp (30 ml) canola oil

2 tbsp fresh dill, finely chopped

3 garlic cloves, grated using
   a Microplane

½ tsp fine sea salt

½ tsp fleur de sel or coarse
   sea salt

○ ○ ○

In a large mixing bowl, whisk together the water, sugar, and salt until most of the sugar and salt have dissolved.

Sprinkle the instant yeast over the water mixture in an even layer. Let sit for 5 minutes to activate. It will go from granulated to foamy, creating a uniform layer on top of the water.

Whisk the mixture until the yeast is incorporated (it's okay if some small clumps remain), then stir in 3 tablespoons (45 ml) of canola oil.

Add ⅓ cup (45 g) of flour, whisking to incorporate. Repeat two more times.

Set the whisk aside. Add ½ cup (70 g) of flour and stir with a wooden spoon to incorporate. Repeat two more times.

Pour ¼ cup (60 ml) of canola oil into a small bowl.

Sprinkle ¼ cup (35 g) of flour over the dough and incorporate using your hands.

Oil your hands (using the oil in the small bowl) and knead the dough directly in the bowl (or on a clean lightly floured work surface, if you prefer). If the dough is very sticky, add the remaining ¼ cup (35 g) of flour, 1 tablespoon (9 g) at a time, kneading between additions. Make sure to oil your hands often to help keep the dough smooth and airy. If you add too much flour, it will be too dense. Once the dough is no longer sticky, but smooth, elastic, and soft, knead for 5 more minutes.

CONTINUED ➤

Remove the dough from the bowl and brush some oil onto the bottom and sides of the bowl.

Cover the dough in a thin layer of oil, return it to the bowl, and cover it with plastic wrap or a clean kitchen towel. Let rise for 1 hour in a warm environment.

Dust a clean work surface with flour and grease a 9-inch pie dish with canola oil or cooking spray.

Transfer the dough to your work surface and sprinkle lightly with flour. Using your hands, form the dough into a 14-inch log. Cut it into 15 equal pieces. To form into balls, pull each dough piece outward, then gather the edges together under the dome and pinch together. If you find that the dough is too sticky, making it hard to form each ball, dust each ball with a little flour.

Place in the glass dish, smooth side up. Brush canola oil over the pampushki or spray with cooking spray. Loosely cover in plastic wrap (you can reuse the piece you used previously). Let rise for 15 minutes in a warm environment.

Meanwhile, preheat the oven to 350°F.

For the garlicky glaze, mix together the water, canola oil, dill, grated garlic, and fine sea salt in a small bowl. Set aside.

Bake the rolls for 25 to 30 minutes, until they turn brown. To add a deeper brown color, broil at 500°F for 1 to 2 minutes after baking.

Remove from the oven, give the garlicky glaze a stir, and immediately spoon over the hot rolls. Garnish with fleur de sel.

Enjoy warm or at room temperature. Store at room temperature, tightly covered with foil, for up to 2 days.

Deep-Fried Oyster Mushrooms with Tangy Aioli

(GLUTEN-FREE OPTION)

(NUT/SEED-FREE) (EXTRA PREP)

MAKES: 4 SERVINGS
PREPARATION: 20 MINUTES
COOKING: 30 MINUTES

○ ○

⅓ cup all-purpose flour (see note)

1 tsp dried onion or onion powder

¾ tsp sea salt

½ tsp black pepper

½ tsp sweet paprika

½ cup + 2 tbsp water

2 cups panko (see note)

8 oz (227 g) oyster mushrooms

4 cups canola oil, for frying

Tangy Aioli (p. 259), for serving

Lemon wedges, for serving, optional

○

I RARELY DEEP-FRY at home. Not because I don't like fried food (I actually *love it*), but because I just don't love having to handle that much oil and washing everything up afterward. Therefore, most of my fried food comes from restaurants. But I just *had* to include a handful of recipes in this book that celebrates the deliciousness of crispy, golden-brown foods cooked in hot oil and served with a creamy sauce. These fried oyster mushrooms are inspired by one of the fried items on menus that would, without fail, grab my attention: fried calamari. To bring the mushrooms to life, you will have to first dip them in a spiced batter, then coat them with panko, making sure to handle them with care to avoid any breakage. The last (and most crucial) step involves frying the mushrooms—be fully present here to ensure your oil reaches the right temperature and that your mushrooms to do not turn overly brown in color.

○ ○ ○

In a mixing bowl, whisk together the flour, dried onion, salt, pepper, and paprika to combine. Whisk in the water until fully combined.

Place the panko in a separate mixing bowl.

Use your hands to break the mushrooms into pieces about 3 inches long and ½ to 1 inch wide.

Arrange the bowls in front of you in this order, from left to right: the panko, the flour mixture, and the mushrooms. Place an empty plate to the left of the panko.

Using your right hand, drop a piece of mushroom into the flour mixture. Using your right hand, carefully toss it to coat, then hold it over the bowl and let any excess batter drip off. Next, gently drop it in the bowl with the panko.

Now, using your left hand, lightly coat the mushroom in panko, then transfer it to the plate.

Repeat the process with the remaining mushroom pieces.

CONTINUED ➤

Preheat the oven to 200°F. Line a large plate or baking sheet with paper towel and place in the oven.

Pour the canola oil into a pot. Alternatively, you can use a skillet—just make sure it's deep enough that the mushrooms don't touch the bottom while frying. Heat the canola oil over medium-high heat to between 350°F and 375°F—test it with a kitchen thermometer. If you don't have a thermometer, carefully sprinkle the oil with a few drops of water: if the oil bubbles vigorously, it's ready for frying.

Using chopsticks, carefully place a few pieces of mushrooms in the oil, making sure not to overcrowd the pan.

Fry the mushrooms until they're golden brown, about 5 minutes, turning them on their sides to help with even cooking and browning. I like to use the chopsticks to move the mushrooms around. Remove from the oil and place on the prepared plate or baking sheet in the oven to keep warm.

Repeat the process with the remaining mushroom pieces.

Enjoy while still warm with the aioli and a squeeze of lemon, if desired.

NOTE:

For a gluten-free version, swap the all-purpose flour with gluten-free all-purpose flour and the panko with gluten-free panko.

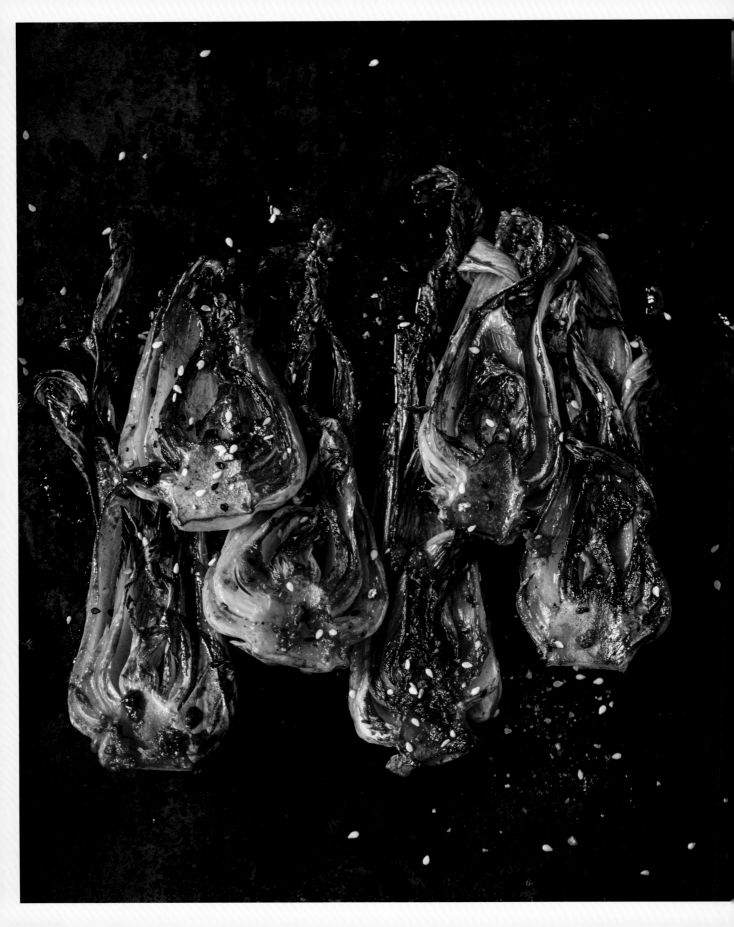

Garlicky Miso-Glazed Bok Choy

(GLUTEN-FREE) (NUT/SEED-FREE)

MAKES: 4 SERVINGS
PREPARATION: 5 MINUTES
COOKING: 10 MINUTES

BOK CHOY IS such an underrated vegetable. As someone who is not a huge fan of greens in general, I have to admit that bok choy is actually a favorite food of mine. I have it for dinner at least once a week because it's incredibly quick and easy to prepare. Don't let the speed of this recipe fool you, though—you have to be fully present for this one, as it is very easy to overcook bok choy. This dish is what I would call the Lamborghini of bok choy—not necessarily because the ingredients are expensive, but because it tastes like a restaurant-worthy appetizer. The mixture of umami miso, salty tamari, tangy rice vinegar, spicy garlic, sweet maple syrup, and zesty lemon elevate the bok choy to new heights!

3 garlic cloves, grated using a Microplane

1 tbsp dark miso

1 tbsp tamari

1 tbsp rice vinegar

1 tsp maple syrup

Zest of ½ a lemon

½ tsp ground black pepper

1½ tbsp avocado oil

4 bok choy, halved lengthwise

Black and white sesame seeds, for garnish

In a bowl, whisk together the garlic, miso, tamari, rice vinegar, maple syrup, lemon zest, and pepper. Set aside.

Heat the avocado oil in a large pan set over medium heat. Add the bok choy, cut side down. Cover with a lid and let steam for 4 minutes or until the bok choy leaves are softened and are a vibrant green color.

Remove the lid and let the bok choy cook for another 3 minutes, without tossing it, to allow its water to evaporate and to give some color to the bottom half of each piece.

Increase the heat to high, spoon the garlicky sauce over the bok choy, and cook for 1 minute. Give the bok choy a toss, then continue cooking until most of the liquid has evaporated and the cut side of the bok choy is caramelized.

Sprinkle with the sesame seeds and serve immediately.

NOTE:

I find that bok choy is best eaten straight away once cooked, so I always use my biggest pan to make this recipe to ensure that all the halves are cooked evenly and ready at the same time.

Most weeknights, I tend to improvise dinner. I put together simple, nutritious meals based on what I have on hand. However, when the weekend comes around, I love consciously slowing down and treating myself to a more luxurious meal. It does not have to be complex or take long to put together, but I strive to create an experience out of my time in the kitchen: carefully picking a recipe, sourcing its ingredients, slowly prepping them, and making my way through the instructions, with attention and care.

I have also been converted these past few years, thanks to my husband, to meal prepping larger quantities of food, which allows me not only to be present while cooking but also to extend the pleasure of enjoying leftovers prepared with love on a later day.

As you discover this chapter's recipes, notice the little hints I have sprinkled throughout about how *you* can make your cooking experience a more mindful one.

Marvelous
Main Dishes

Veggie Rice

GLUTEN-FREE   NUT/SEED-FREE

MAKES: 4–6 SERVINGS
PREPARATION: 5 MINUTES
COOKING: 1 HOUR

○

WHEN I THINK OF Congolese dishes from my childhood, I often think of ones that are layered in flavor yet still simple to make. This rice dish is just that. Although it's not a traditional Congolese recipe, it's inspired by rice dishes I grew up eating, many of which were one-pot dishes that featured various vegetables and at least one legume. Here, the rich flavor comes from treating the ingredients with love by cooking them in stages (caramelizing the onion and carrot, adding garlic and spices to allow the flavors to bloom) before assembling and giving everything ample time to cook together as a whole. Don't omit the Scotch bonnet: it's the star that pulls everything together to give this veggie rice its unique flavor. This dish is perfect for busy weeknights or even to prep up to 1 week ahead.

○ ○

2 tbsp avocado oil

1 onion, diced

1 carrot, peeled and cut in ½-inch cubes

1 red or orange bell pepper, coarsely chopped

3 garlic cloves, minced

½ tsp smoked paprika

½ tsp ground ginger

½ tsp ground cinnamon

1 cup brown basmati rice, rinsed

1½ cups black beans, from a can, drained and rinsed

½ Scotch bonnet pepper, coarsely chopped (see note)

2 cups coarsely chopped beefsteak or Roma tomatoes

2 cups vegetable broth or vegan chicken broth

½ tsp sea salt

○ ○ ○

In a large heavy-bottomed pot or a Dutch oven, heat the avocado oil over medium heat. Add the onion and carrot and cook for about 5 minutes, stirring occasionally with a wooden spoon, until the onion is translucent and starting to caramelize around the edges.

Stir in the bell pepper, garlic, paprika, ginger, and cinnamon. Cook for 1 minute.

Add the rice, black beans, Scotch bonnet, tomatoes, broth, and salt. Give the mixture a good stir, increase the heat to high, and bring to a boil. Reduce the heat to low, cover, and cook for 40 to 45 minutes, until all the liquid has been absorbed.

Turn off the heat and let the rice sit on the stovetop, covered, for 5 minutes. Stir with a wooden spoon to ensure everything is mixed together, then enjoy.

Store in the fridge in an airtight container for up to 5 days.

NOTE:

If you do not do well with spiciness, make sure to remove the seeds from the Scotch bonnet pepper. You could also use only a quarter of the pepper.

Saka Saka

(GLUTEN-FREE) (EXTRA PREP)

MAKES: 4 SERVINGS
PREPARATION: 15 MINUTES
COOKING: 2 HOURS

YOU HAVE NO IDEA how long I'd been dreaming of this recipe before attempting it. Saka Saka is a stew I grew up eating in Congo and in which I indulge in during family gatherings on my dad's side. This is the kind of dish in which flavors unravel exponentially with time. As you let the greens, the garlic, the peppers, the onions, and the peanut butter all cook down together, it's as if a rainbow of flavors starts to appear. Funnily enough, it's only when I became vegan that I got the urge to try cooking it myself, making it plant-based by leaving out the fish of the traditional dish. I am so glad I did try it, because now I can share this incredible recipe that is near and dear to my heart. I hope that you too will fall in love with it! You can serve this stew with white rice or Coconut Rice (p. 100), Pan-Fried Plantains (p. 103), and Fufu (p. 118).

1 tbsp avocado oil

1 cup diced red onion

4 garlic cloves, minced

1 large green bell pepper, diced

2½ cups cassava leaves (a 18 oz/500 g frozen package), thawed and drained

2½ packed cups (4½ oz/125 g) fresh spinach

¼ habanero pepper, chopped (see note)

2½ cups vegetable broth or vegan chicken broth

½ tsp sea salt, plus more to taste

¼ tsp black pepper, plus more to taste

2 green onions, chopped

3 tbsp natural crunchy or smooth peanut butter

GARNISHES (OPTIONAL)

Chopped peanuts

Hot sauce, such as sambal oelek

Finely chopped parsley or green onion

Heat a large saucepan over medium heat. Add the avocado oil and onion and cook, stirring occasionally with a wooden spoon, for 7 to 8 minutes, until the onion is translucent and starting to brown.

Add the garlic and bell pepper, and cook for 1 minute.

Stir in the cassava leaves, spinach, habanero, broth, salt, and pepper.

Bring the mixture to a boil over high heat, then reduce the heat to low and cook for 1 hour 30 minutes, covered, stirring occasionally.

Add the green onions and peanut butter. Stir and let simmer, uncovered, for 15 minutes.

Taste and adjust the seasonings to your liking.

Garnish with peanuts, hot sauce, and parsley. Serve hot alongside coconut rice, pan-fried plantains, and fufu.

Store in the fridge in an airtight container for up to 5 days.

NOTE:

Depending on your heat tolerance, the amount of habanero pepper can really vary. If you are super sensitive to heat, simply skip it in this recipe or use a quarter but remove the seeds. On the other hand, if you love the heat, you can use half or an entire habanero pepper, seeds included.

Smoky Sweet Potato Mac and Cheese

(GLUTEN-FREE) (NUT/SEED-FREE)

MAKES: 4 SERVINGS
PREPARATION: 10 MINUTES
COOKING: 20 MINUTES

IF YOU ARE looking for a nut-free, flavor-packed mac and cheese, you are in luck! This recipe came to me when I was looking for a relatively quick and protein-packed meal for my workout days. I wanted something that would fill me up but was not the traditional bean, rice, and veggie bowls I eat during most of the workweek. Unlike with many other vegan mac and cheese recipes, this sauce doesn't use cashews or store-bought vegan cheese, nor require multiple veggies. The simple base of sweet potatoes is elevated using key ingredients and spices, which all come together to create a bowl of pure goodness. I encourage you, as you make the sauce, to taste it and notice how every addition plays a role in creating flavor, and to not hesitate to adjust the seasonings to your liking.

○ ○

2 tbsp extra virgin olive oil

1 onion, diced

3 garlic cloves

1½ cups cooked and peeled sweet potato (see note)

1¼ cups unsweetened soy milk

¼ cup + 1 tbsp nutritional yeast

4 pickled banana pepper rings, plus more to taste

3 tbsp banana pepper pickle juice

½ tsp chili powder, plus more to taste

½ tsp apple cider vinegar

¼ tsp smoked paprika

¼ tsp garlic powder

2¼ tsp sea salt, divided, plus more to taste

Black pepper, to taste

2½ cups lentil elbow pasta (see note)

○ ○ ○

Heat the olive oil in a large saucepan set over medium heat. Add the onion and cook, stirring often to prevent burning, for 5 minutes or until the onion is translucent and starting to caramelize.

Add the garlic and cook for 1 minute.

Transfer the mixture to a high-speed blender and add the sweet potatoes, soy milk, nutritional yeast, banana pepper rings and their juice, chili powder, apple cider vinegar, paprika, garlic powder, ¼ teaspoon of salt, and pepper. Blend until smooth.

Taste and adjust the salt, pepper, banana pepper, or chili powder to your liking. Set the mixture aside.

Fill the same large saucepan with water. Add the remaining 2 teaspoons of salt and bring to a boil over high heat.

Cook the pasta until it's al dente, following the package instructions. Reserve 1 cup of pasta water, then drain the pasta and return to the empty pot.

Reduce the heat to medium-low. Pour the sauce overtop the pasta and stir to coat. Heat for a few minutes to warm the sauce to your liking. If the sauce thickens too much for your liking, add 1 tablespoon of pasta water at a time to thin it.

CONTINUED ➤

Date-Sweetened Leek and Onion Jam (p. 270), for garnish, optional

Chili flakes, for garnish, optional

Fresh parsley, for garnish, optional

Transfer the mac and cheese to individual plates or bowls and garnish with leek and onion jam, a crack of pepper, a sprinkle of chili flakes, and parsley, if desired.

Store the leftovers in the fridge in an airtight container for up to 2 days.

NOTES:

To cook the unpeeled sweet potato, poke it with a fork a dozen times, then microwave it for 7 to 10 minutes on high power, or bake it in the oven at 425°F for 1 hour or until fork-tender.

I often use lentil pasta to bulk up this dish, making it more filling and giving it extra protein. Feel free to swap it for regular, whole-wheat, or gluten-free pasta.

Saucy Eggplant "Chicken"

(GLUTEN-FREE) (NUT/SEED-FREE)

MAKES: 4–6 SERVINGS
PREPARATION: 10 MINUTES
COOKING: 30 MINUTES

WHEN MY MOM first made this dish for my youngest brother (who not only is not vegan but has an aversion to vegan foods), he never noticed that it was 100% plant-based. He actually thought the eggplant was chicken, which is why we started calling this dish Eggplant Chicken. Sautéing the eggplants causes them to go from pale and firm to beautifully caramelized, with an almost melt-in-your-mouth quality. This process takes some time and attention, but I love noticing the eggplant's slow transformation. Things get even better when it's tossed with bell peppers, lightly cooked onion, and a bright umami-vinegary sauce. I promise you, this recipe can convince any skeptic of the amazingness of eggplant. Serve this dish alongside brown rice, Coconut Rice (p. 100), or even my Ultimate Mashed Potatoes (p. 104).

○ ○

2 eggplants, peeled and cut in 1-inch cubes

⅓ cup + 2 tsp cornstarch, divided

¼ cup + 1 tbsp avocado oil, divided

1 tbsp water

1 onion, halved lengthwise, then quartered

3 garlic cloves, minced

½ red chili pepper, finely chopped, optional

2 coarsely chopped bell peppers (I like to use a mix of colors)

UMAMI SAUCE

2 chopped green onions (green and white parts)

1 garlic clove, grated using a Microplane

¼ cup tamari

¼ cup rice vinegar

1 tbsp + 1 tsp maple syrup

1½ tsp sesame oil

○ ○ ○

In a large bowl, toss the eggplants in ⅓ cup of cornstarch to coat.

Heat ¼ cup of avocado oil in a large pan (I use an 11-inch pan) over medium heat. Cook the eggplants until golden brown and caramelized on all sides, about 20 to 25 minutes. Toss often using a silicone spatula. Transfer to a paper towel–lined plate, reserving the pan (no need to clean).

In a small bowl, stir the water and the remaining 2 teaspoons of cornstarch together until the cornstarch has dissolved. Set aside.

For the umami sauce, in a bowl, whisk together all the sauce ingredients. Set aside.

Heat the same pan over medium heat, add the remaining 1 tablespoon of oil, onion, garlic, and red chili pepper, if using. Cook for 1 to 2 minutes, tossing constantly, until the onion starts to become translucent. Be careful not to burn the garlic.

Add the bell peppers and sauté for 1 minute, tossing constantly.

Add the eggplant and sauté for 1 minute. Pour in the sauce and cook for another minute. Finally, give the cornstarch mixture a good stir to make sure the cornstarch is fully dissolved and pour into the pan with the veggies.

CONTINUED ➤

Sliced green onions, for garnish,
   optional

Sesame seeds, for garnish,
   optional

Stir and cook for 2 more minutes or until the sauce has thickened and all the veggies are coated with it.

Serve alongside your grain of choice, topped with green onions and a sprinkling of sesame seeds. Store leftovers in the fridge in an airtight container for up to 2 days.

NOTE:

Although this stew is not overly spicy, if you are very sensitive to heat, omit the habanero and the cayenne. You can also just use the flesh of the habanero and discard the seeds.

Peanut Butter and Sweet Potato Stew

(GLUTEN-FREE)

MAKES: 6 SERVINGS
PREPARATION: 5 MINUTES
COOKING: 1 HOUR

THE VERY FIRST TIME I had peanut butter in a savory recipe was when my mother-in-law used it in a rich, ultra-fragrant peanut butter chicken stew. The flavor was so divine, it inspired this recipe. I opted for tofu as the main protein source, grilling it on a cast-iron grill pan to add beautiful grill marks and a touch smokiness. The stew itself is cooked in vegan chicken broth and tomatoes, and seasoned with aromatic garlic, ginger, habanero, and coriander. The sweet potatoes bring out an extra layer of flavor, adding a natural sweetness that beautifully complements the peanut butter's richness and the tomatoes' acidity. Serve alongside Coconut Rice (p. 100) and Fufu (p. 118) for a complete meal.

1 (1 lb/454 g) package extra-firm tofu, cut in 1-inch cubes

2 tbsp canola oil, divided, plus more for greasing

¼ tsp cayenne pepper

½–1 tsp sea salt, plus more to taste

1 large onion, chopped

1 large sweet potato, peeled and cut in ½-inch cubes

4 garlic cloves, minced

½ habanero, finely chopped

2 tbsp grated ginger

2 tsp ground coriander

1½ cups crushed or strained tomatoes from a can

2 cups vegan chicken broth or vegetable broth

½ cup natural crunchy or smooth peanut butter

2 packed cups Lacinato or curly kale, cut in bite-sized pieces

Chopped fresh coriander, for garnish

In a mixing bowl, mix together the tofu, 1 tablespoon of canola oil, cayenne, and a generous pinch of salt with a silicone spatula, coating the tofu.

Heat a grill pan or frying pan over medium heat. Brush some oil onto the pan or spray with cooking spray.

Arrange the tofu on the pan so that the pieces are not touching each other. Cook, turning using a fork, for 15 minutes or until all sides of the tofu have grill marks on them (or until golden, if using a frying pan). Remove from the heat and set aside.

Heat a large pot over medium heat. Add the remaining 1 tablespoon of oil and the onion and cook, stirring occasionally, for 5 to 7 minutes, until the onion is translucent and starting to brown.

Add the sweet potatoes, stir, and cook for 5 minutes. Stir in the garlic, habanero, if using, ginger, and coriander. Cook for 1 minute. Stir in the tomatoes, broth, and grilled tofu. Increase the heat to high and bring to a boil, uncovered.

Cover, reduce the heat to low, and simmer for 25 to 35 minutes, until the sweet potato is fork-tender. Stir in the peanut butter, ¼ teaspoon of salt, and the kale. Cook, uncovered, until the kale has softened. Taste and add more salt to your liking.

Serve warm, garnished with fresh coriander. Store leftovers in the fridge in an airtight container for up to 5 days.

The Burger for the Non-vegans

(CUSTOMIZABLE)

(GLUTEN-FREE OPTION)

(NUT/SEED-FREE) (EXTRA PREP)

MAKES: 4 SERVINGS
PREPARATION: 10 MINUTES
COOKING: 20 MINUTES

IF YOU HAVE a family member who's not convinced that a vegan burger can be just as good as a meat burger—or if you are that person yourself—I just *have* to try to convince you otherwise with this recipe. These burgers feature a few store-bought ingredients, but that doesn't mean you can't add your own personality and favorite toppings to them. I jazzed mine up with spicy mayo, tangy pickles, and fresh veggies. As you put these burgers together, I encourage you to do it consciously and reflect on how each ingredient brings forth flavor and/or texture. And have fun with it! I truly think burgers are one of the best ways to explore new flavor profiles and get creative with ingredients (I mean, some restaurants even put mac and cheese in their burgers!).

4 store-bought vegan onion rings (see note)

4 vegan store-bought brioche buns (see note)

Unsalted vegan butter, optional

4 vegan patties (I like Beyond Meat)

4 slices of vegan cheddar cheese

¼ cup Homemade Mayo (p. 258) or store-bought vegan mayonnaise

1 tbsp hot sauce, such as sambal oelek or sriracha

Ketchup

4 pieces curly lettuce (I like green leaf lettuce)

4 slices of tomato

8 slices of Tofu Bacon (p. 59), warm

Sliced dill pickles

Garlicky Roasted Potatoes (p. 106), for serving

Preheat the oven to 425°F. Line a baking sheet with parchment paper or a silicone mat.

Bake the onion rings according to the package instructions.

Meanwhile, in a large pan set over medium heat, toast the brioche buns, face down. For extra decadence, spread a bit of butter onto each half before toasting. Remove from the pan and set aside.

Add the patties to the pan. Flip when caramelized and browned on the bottom, then top each with a slice of the vegan cheddar. Cover the pan and cook the patties until the bottoms are brown and the cheese is melted.

In a small bowl, prepare the spicy mayo by mixing together the mayo and hot sauce. Spread the spicy mayo on the bun bottoms. Spread some ketchup on the bun tops.

Top each of the bottom buns with a piece of lettuce, a patty, a tomato slice, 2 slices of tofu bacon, dill pickles, and an onion ring. Close the burger.

Best eaten fresh alongside garlicky roasted potatoes.

NOTE:

When shopping for store-bought onion rings or brioche buns, check to make sure they contain no dairy or milk ingredients.

Veggie-Loaded Pizza

(CUSTOMIZABLE)

(GLUTEN-FREE OPTION)

(NUT/SEED-FREE) (EXTRA PREP)

MAKES: 4–6 SERVINGS
PREPARATION: 15 MINUTES
COOKING: 1 HOUR 20 MINUTES

○

THIS PIZZA IS a perfect Friday or Saturday night cooking opportunity! I love getting ready to prepare it by sourcing all my ingredients, and planning my night around making it. The day of the preparation, I put on my favorite *Dancing in the Kitchen* playlist and start the preparation process: roasting the garlic and eggplant, sautéing the mushrooms, and rolling out the dough. When I feel extra celebratory, the process also features a glass of red wine. By the time the pizza is out of the oven and garnished with sun-dried tomatoes, arugula, and a balsamic reduction, I am in a happy, peaceful place knowing that I put so much love into bringing this dish to life—and excited to share it with whichever loved one is with me that night.

○ ○

ROASTED GARLIC AND EGGPLANT

1 garlic head

Olive oil

Sea salt and black pepper, to taste

1 eggplant

Cooking spray

PIZZA CRUST

1 lb/454 g store-bought pizza
   dough, thawed (see note)

SAUTÉED MUSHROOMS

2 tsp avocado oil

1 small onion, diced

4 oz (115 g) button mushrooms,
   sliced

2 garlic cloves, minced

Sea salt and black pepper, to taste

○ ○ ○

PREPARE THE ROASTED GARLIC AND EGGPLANT

Preheat the oven to 400°F. Line a baking sheet with parchment paper.

Cut about ¼ inch off the top of the garlic head and place it on a piece of foil. Lightly drizzle with olive oil and season with salt and pepper. Wrap the foil tightly around the garlic. Set aside.

Cut off the stem end of the eggplant and peel 4 vertical strips (1 inch apart) of the skin; discard. Slice the eggplant into ¼-inch-thick discs and place on the prepared baking sheet.

Generously spray one side of the eggplant slices with cooking spray, then flip and spray the other side. Alternatively, you can brush oil onto each side. Season lightly with salt and pepper.

Place the foil-wrapped garlic on the baking sheet and bake it and the eggplant for 30 minutes or until the eggplant is golden brown, flipping the slices halfway through the baking time.

Remove the eggplant from the oven. Set the slices on a plate and discard the parchment paper you cooked them on. Place the wrapped garlic directly on the oven rack and roast for an additional 10 minutes. Then remove from the oven and set aside, leaving the oven on.

CONTINUED ➤

PIZZA SAUCE

¼ cup seasoned tomato paste

¼ cup water

TOPPINGS AND GARNISHES

½ loosely packed cup baby
   arugula, plus more for garnish

¼ cup pitted Kalamata olives,
   chopped

¼ packed cup drained sun-dried
   tomatoes in oil, chopped

½ cup shredded or crumbled
   vegan cheese of choice (I like
   vegan feta)

Balsamic reduction, optional
   (see note)

PREPARE THE PIZZA CRUST

Place the pizza dough on a large piece of parchment paper. Cover with another large piece of parchment paper and roll it out into a rectangle of about 10- × 14-inch inches.

Carefully remove the top sheet of parchment and transfer the dough, still on the bottom sheet of parchment, onto the same baking sheet you used for your eggplant slices.

If you want the crust slightly bigger, wet your fingertips, then use them to spread out the dough a little more at the edges.

Poke the crust with a fork all over, about 2 dozen times. Bake for 15 minutes or until the bottom is starting to brown. Remove from the oven and leave on the baking sheet.

SAUTÉ THE MUSHROOMS AND PREPARE THE TOMATO SAUCE

Heat a large pan with the avocado oil over medium heat. Add the onion. Sauté for 5 minutes or until the onion has softened and is starting to caramelize.

Add the mushrooms, increase the heat to medium-high, and cook for 5 minutes, stirring occasionally, until the mushrooms are caramelized.

Add the garlic, and season the mushrooms with salt and pepper. Cook for 2 minutes, then remove from the heat and set aside.

PREPARE THE PIZZA SAUCE

Prepare the pizza sauce by mixing together the tomato paste and water in a small bowl.

ASSEMBLE THE PIZZA

Peel the skin off each of the garlic cloves and discard. Alternatively, you can squeeze the garlic out of its peel, one clove at a time. Evenly spread the garlic on your pizza crust (it will have the texture of a paste) using the back of a spoon or a knife.

Top the roasted garlic with the pizza sauce.

Halve or quarter the eggplant slices and arrange them on your pizza.

Top with ½ cup of arugula, the sautéed mushrooms, olives, sun-dried tomatoes, and cheese.

Bake in the 400°F oven for 10 minutes.

Remove the pizza from the oven and garnish with fresh arugula, a drizzle of balsamic reduction, and a crack of pepper. This pizza is best eaten fresh, but you can store it in the fridge in an airtight container for up to 2 days and reheat in the oven at 400°F for 5 minutes or until heated through.

NOTES:

You can customize this pizza as much as you like by swapping out some of the vegetables for any of your favorites or adding vegan meats and pickled elements such as banana peppers.

Make this recipe gluten-free by using your favorite gluten-free dough (such as a mix by Simple Mills).

I love to use Nonna Pia's Classic Balsamic Glaze, but you can make your own balsamic reduction. Bring to a boil, in a small saucepan, 1 cup of balsamic vinegar. Decrease the heat to low, and simmer, stirring often using a wooden spoon or silicone spatula, until reduced and thickened to your liking (about 10 minutes). Note that it will continue to thicken after it has cooled. Let cool before using or storing. Transfer to a jar and store in the fridge for up to 2 months. If it hardens too much, place the jar in a bowl of warm water to liquefy the glaze before using.

Saucy White Kidney Beans

(GLUTEN-FREE) (NUT/SEED-FREE)

MAKES: 4 SERVINGS
PREPARATION: 5 MINUTES
COOKING: 25 MINUTES
RESTING: 30 MINUTES

FRAGRANT AND SUBTLY FLAVORED, saucy and satisfying, this bean dish is my dad's absolute favorite. He makes a big batch of it on Sundays and enjoys it throughout the week. The dish reminds me of gatherings I used to attend at my dad's church in Canada, where at least one person would bring a variation of it. Some people made it with kidney beans, others incorporated meat; some versions were spicy and others quite mild—giving all who partook of it a little insight into the culinary history and personality of each cook. A lot of the flavor in this recipe comes from the canned tomatoes, which means you don't need to think too much about seasoning (except for salt and pepper, of course!). This dish is great as a main and pairs well with many other sides in this book, including Stewed Greens (p. 117), Pan-Fried Plantains (p. 103), Coconut Rice (p. 100), and Fufu (p. 118).

3 tbsp canola oil

1 cup diced tomatoes with herbs and spices, from a can

3 green onions, sliced

1 large Roma tomato, cubed

½ onion, diced

2 garlic cloves, minced

2 cups cooked white kidney (cannellini) beans, drained and rinsed (see note)

½ cup water

½ tsp sea salt, plus more to taste

Black pepper, to taste

Heat the canola oil in a large saucepan set over medium-high heat.

Add the diced tomatoes, green onions, Roma tomato, onion, and minced garlic to the oil. Stir, cover, and bring to a boil.

Reduce the heat to medium-low and add the kidney beans and water. Stir, cover, and let simmer until all the foam created from the cooking of the beans is gone (about 20 to 25 minutes), stirring occasionally.

Season with the salt and pepper.

Remove from the heat and let rest, covered, for 30 minutes (see note) before enjoying alongside my Stewed Greens (p. 117) and your grain of choice.

Store in the fridge in an airtight container for up to 5 days.

NOTES:

For this recipe, you can either use canned beans or beans you have soaked overnight and cooked yourself on the stovetop or in a pressure cooker.

Although you can totally enjoy this dish immediately, I recommend letting it sit for 30 minutes after cooking. This allows the beans to absorb even more of the liquid, resulting in a thicker stew rather than one with a soup-like consistency.

My Mom's Borscht

(GLUTEN-FREE) (NUT/SEED-FREE)
(EXTRA PREP)

MAKES: 6 SERVINGS
PREPARATION: 15 MINUTES
COOKING: 35 MINUTES
RESTING: 1 HOUR

○

THIS RECIPE IS an ode to my mom and the incredible borscht she's been making for decades. It's changed over time, but its original soul and flavors remain. According to my mom, a borscht needs some key ingredients: beets, carrots, onions, potatoes, cabbage, and tomatoes. From there, the possibilities are endless. What infuses my mom's version with complexity is the caramelizing of the beets, carrots, and onion first, instead of boiling them together with the broth. My mom's advice for this recipe: spend your time with each vegetable, grating, chopping, and slicing before you start cooking—it relieves stress, allowing you to enjoy the process. Serve this dish on its own or with vegan sour cream, fresh dill, and a slice of my No-Knead Overnight Dutch Oven Bread (p. 63) to instantly be transported to my family home.

○ ○

3 tbsp canola oil, divided

1 large carrot, peeled and grated

1 onion, diced

2 garlic cloves, minced

Sea salt, to taste

Black pepper, to taste

1 small beet, peeled and grated

¾ cup passata (strained tomatoes) or canned crushed tomatoes, unseasoned

5–6 cups hot vegetable broth or vegan beef broth

1 large Yukon Gold potato, cut in ½-inch cubes

1 bay leaf

1 red bell pepper, cored and thinly sliced lengthwise

¼ small green cabbage, cored and thinly sliced

○ ○ ○

Heat 2 tablespoons of canola oil in a large pot set over medium heat. Add the grated carrot and cook, stirring often with a wooden spoon, for 5 to 6 minutes, until the pieces have become slightly desaturated in color and start to turn golden around the edges.

Add the onion and cook, stirring often, for 4 to 5 minutes, until the onion is translucent. Sprinkle in the minced garlic and season with generous pinches of salt and pepper. Transfer to a plate or bowl.

Return the pot to the stovetop, add the remaining 1 tablespoon of oil, and heat over medium heat. Add the grated beet and cook for 4 minutes or until the beet juice has mostly been cooked out of the beet. Pour in the passata and cook for 3 minutes.

Pour in 5 cups of vegetable broth, the potato, and bay leaf. Increase the heat to high and bring to a boil. Reduce the heat to medium and cook, uncovered, for 8 to 10 minutes, until the potatoes are fork-tender but still hold their shape.

Add the bell pepper, cabbage, white beans, and carrot mixture. If you want a thinner borscht, feel free to add the additional broth at this stage. Increase the heat to bring the borscht to a boil, then reduce the heat to medium-low and cook for 3 minutes.

CONTINUED ➤

1 cup cooked white beans (such as white kidney or navy beans), drained and rinsed (see note)

Chili flakes, optional

Vegan sour cream, for serving, optional

Fresh dill, for serving, optional

No-Knead Overnight Dutch Oven Bread (p. 63), for serving, optional

Taste and adjust salt and pepper levels. Sprinkle in chili flakes for an extra kick, if desired. Turn off the heat. Cover and leave on the stovetop for at least 1 hour or until ready to eat.

Enjoy the soup topped with vegan sour cream and fresh dill, along with slices of bread, if you like. Store leftovers in the fridge in an airtight container for up to 1 week—trust me, the flavors develop even more after just 24 hours.

NOTE:

You can either use canned beans or beans you have soaked overnight and cooked yourself on the stovetop or in a pressure cooker.

All-Green Gnocchi with Vegan Pesto

MAKES: 4 SERVINGS
PREPARATION: 30 MINUTES
COOKING: 30 MINUTES

○

COLORED WITH FRESH SPINACH, these light and pillowy gnocchi are coated with a bright and fragrant plant-based pesto. Requiring only a few ingredients (including many that you probably already have in your cupboards) and no special tools, these gnocchi are a wonderful alternative to store-bought pasta. Do not rush when making this recipe. Enjoy the process of mashing the potatoes, incorporating the flour, and witnessing the color change to a vibrant green, thanks to the spinach puree. Have fun forming the dough into logs, then into little balls, and watching them float up to the water's surface during boiling. Making homemade pasta is an extremely satisfying and rewarding process. In this case, the result is an herbaceous, tangy, and luxurious dish.

○ ○

PESTO

3 garlic cloves

1 packed cup fresh basil

¼ packed cup chives

¼ cup (40 g) hemp hearts

¼ cup (20 g) nutritional yeast

¼ cup (60 ml) extra virgin olive oil

2–3 tbsp (30–45 ml) lemon juice, divided

½ tsp sea salt, plus more to taste

Black pepper, to taste

○ ○ ○

PREPARE THE PESTO

In a food processor, pulse the garlic, basil, chives, hemp hearts, nutritional yeast, olive oil, 2 tablespoons (30 ml) of lemon juice, and salt until the garlic and herbs are finely chopped. Taste, season with salt and pepper, and add 1 more tablespoon (15 ml) of lemon juice, if desired. Set aside.

PREPARE THE GNOCCHI

To a large pot of water, add the potatoes and 1 teaspoon of salt. Cover and bring to a boil over high heat.

Reduce the heat to medium and cook, partly covered, for 10 to 15 minutes, until the potatoes are fork-tender.

Drain, transfer to a large bowl, and let cool until cool enough to handle. Mash until smooth.

Meanwhile, in a tall cup or bowl, blend the spinach, olive oil, and remaining ¼ teaspoon of salt with an immersion blender (alternatively, you can use a mini blender or a mini food processor) until smooth.

CONTINUED ➤

GNOCCHI

1 tsp + ¼ tsp sea salt

3 russet potatoes (23 oz/650 g), peeled and cubed

2 packed cups (2½ oz/70 g) fresh spinach

2 tbsp (30 ml) olive oil

2 cups (280 g) all-purpose flour, plus more as needed

Olive oil, for coating

Grated vegan parmesan, for garnish, optional

Add the spinach mixture to the mashed potatoes and mix with a silicone spatula.

Sprinkle in 2 cups of flour and incorporate using the spatula. Use your hands to form a ball with the dough. If you find that it is too sticky to handle, add more flour, 1 tablespoon (9 g) at a time, until it is no longer sticking to your hands.

Dust a clean work surface with flour and transfer the dough to it. Divide the dough into 16 equal pieces, then return the dough pieces to the bowl, keeping 1 piece to work with. Cover the bowl with a clean kitchen towel.

Have a large plate or baking sheet at the ready.

Use your hands to form the piece of dough you are working with into a log about 12 inches long. Slice the log into 1-inch-thick pieces. Form a ball with each piece by rolling it between your hands. Alternatively, you can leave each piece as is, resembling a square little pillow. Place on the plate.

Repeat the process with the remaining pieces of dough, lightly dusting your work surface with flour each time to prevent the dough from sticking. To prevent the gnocchi from sticking to each other, don't let them touch each other on the plate.

Bring a large pot of salted water to a boil and carefully place one-third of your gnocchi in it. Keep the heat on high.

The gnocchi will float to the surface when they are almost ready. Once they do, let them cook for another minute, then use a slotted spoon to transfer them to a large bowl. Toss in a bit of olive oil to keep them moist.

Repeat the process with the remaining gnocchi, cooking them in two batches.

Pour the pesto over the gnocchi and toss to coat.

Garnish with grated vegan parmesan, if desired, and enjoy warm. Keep any leftovers in the fridge in an airtight container for up to 2 days.

Meaty Thai Green Curry-Spiced Ramen

(CUSTOMIZABLE) (NUT/SEED-FREE)
(GLUTEN-FREE OPTION)

MAKES: 4 SERVINGS
PREPARATION: 5 MINUTES
COOKING: 15 MINUTES

○○

4 (5 oz/140 g each) blocks ramen (I like Lotus Foods's)

Avocado oil

4 plant-based patties, thawed if frozen (I like Beyond Meat)

1 large onion, diced

1 large red or orange bell pepper, coarsely chopped (see note)

4 garlic cloves, minced

¼ cup Thai green curry paste, plus more to taste (I like Thai Kitchen's)

1 cup full-fat coconut milk

2 tbsp tamari, plus more to taste

2 cups (2 oz/60 g) loosely packed baby spinach or kale, stems removed and chopped into bite-sized pieces

Sambal oelek or sriracha, optional

Splash of rice vinegar or lime juice, optional

Sesame seeds, for garnish

Sliced green onions, for garnish

○

THIS RECIPE IS one of my go-tos after a long shoot day. I love it because it is customizable and relatively quick to put together, but also requires me to be present in the cooking process: chopping the veggies, cooking the ramen separately, browning the plant-based patties, and evenly stirring in the coconut milk and chili paste. It's meditative for me, which helps transition my brain from work mode to relax mode. I also love that the ramen noodles are coated in a luscious, rich coconutty sauce flavored with a Thai green curry paste that lends notes of lemongrass, galangal, and, of course, green chilis. It's a dish that feels luxurious and is very satisfying without having to spend hours in the kitchen!

○○○

Cook the ramen according to the package instructions. Drain, transfer to a bowl, and drizzle with a bit of avocado oil. Stir to keep the noodles from sticking together.

Heat a large sauté pan over medium-high heat. Add the patties and onion. Use a wooden spoon to break up the patties and cook, stirring often, until the meat is browned and the onion has softened and is browning at the edges, about 5 minutes.

Reduce the heat to medium, sprinkle in the chopped bell pepper, and cook until softened, about 3 minutes. Add the garlic and green chili paste, stirring until well incorporated. Pour in the coconut milk and tamari, stir, and cook for 1 minute. Add the baby spinach and cook, stirring often, until wilted.

Taste and adjust the seasoning to your liking by adding sambal oelek for heat, a splash of rice vinegar for acidity, more tamari for saltiness, or more green chili paste for depth of flavor.

Add the cooked ramen and stir until coated and everything is evenly distributed. Divide among four individual bowls, garnish with sesame seeds and green onions, and enjoy.

NOTE:

If you don't have bell peppers on hand, swap them out with sliced mushrooms—just be sure to cook the mushrooms until golden brown before adding the garlic and chili paste. You could also use small broccoli florets instead, but make sure not to overcook them.

Spicy Gochujang Tofu

(GLUTEN-FREE) (NUT/SEED-FREE)

MAKES: 4 SERVINGS
PREPARATION: 5 MINUTES
COOKING: 15 MINUTES

THERE WAS A TIME when I would eat tofu at least three times per week. My go-to recipe was by a well-known and incredibly talented Quebec chef, Caroline Huard (also known as Loounie). She has this simple, quick-to-make, tasty recipe called Tofu Magique, which consists of tofu coated in a mixture of lemon juice, tamari, maple syrup, and tons of nutritional yeast. This Spicy Gochujang Tofu is my twist on Caroline's recipe. Although this recipe is quick and easy to execute, I encourage you to not rush the crisping of the tofu, as this will make the biggest difference in the texture of the dish. You can also taste your sauce as you are making it, noticing how each element brings forth another layer of flavor notes, from umami and savory to spicy, sweet, and fermented.

∘ ∘

2 tbsp gochujang

2 garlic gloves, grated using a Microplane

1 tbsp maple syrup

1 tbsp tamari

1 tbsp rice vinegar

1 (1 lb/454 g) package extra-firm tofu, patted dry

2 tbsp cornstarch

2 tbsp nutritional yeast

1 tbsp avocado oil

Sliced green onions, for garnish

Black and white sesame seeds, for garnish

∘ ∘ ∘

In a small bowl, whisk together the gochujang, garlic, maple syrup, tamari, and rice vinegar until the gochujang is fully incorporated. Set aside.

Break the tofu into bite-sized pieces and place in a large mixing bowl. Sprinkle in the cornstarch and nutritional yeast. Toss using a silicone spatula until the tofu is well coated.

Heat the avocado oil in a nonstick pan set over medium-high heat. Add the tofu, leaving behind any excess cornstarch, nutritional yeast, and tiny tofu pieces.

Cook, tossing the tofu often using a silicone spatula, until golden and crispy at the edges, about 7 to 10 minutes.

Reduce the heat to medium. Pour the gochujang mixture over the tofu and cook, tossing, for 1 minute or until the tofu is coated and glistening.

Remove from the heat and garnish with sliced green onions and sesame seeds. Serve hot alongside my Coconut Rice (p. 100) or Garlicky Miso-Glazed Bok Choy (p. 127), or any of your favorite sides.

Store leftovers in the fridge in an airtight container for up to 24 hours.

Sun-Dried Tomato and Caper Orzo

(GLUTEN-FREE OPTION)
(NUT/SEED-FREE)

MAKES: 4–6 SERVINGS
PREPARATION: 10 MINUTES
COOKING: 10 MINUTES

○

MADE WITH A homemade sun-dried tomato pesto, this pasta recipe is bright, salty, and lemony. One of the most comforting dishes, to my mind, is plain pasta with a little olive oil and a touch of pesto. I remember watching my mom as she assembled this very simple dish for us on weeknights, mesmerized as she coated pasta with her bright green pesto. This version is an ode to that meal. While it is quick to put together, I love taking extra care, just like my mom did, to slowly coat the pasta with the flavor-packed sun-dried tomato pesto, noticing how the red hue envelops the dish. This pasta is great eaten hot, but if you have any leftovers, you can store them in the fridge and enjoy cold the next day—or warmed up, of course!

○ ○

SUN-DRIED TOMATO PESTO

1 loosely packed cup sun-dried tomatoes in oil, drained

3 garlic cloves

2 tbsp capers, drained

2 tbsp nutritional yeast

2 tbsp olive oil

1 tbsp lemon juice

2 tsp tomato paste

Black pepper, to taste

PASTA

1 (1 lb/454 g) package orzo (see note)

Chopped parsley, for garnish, optional

Chopped capers, for garnish, optional

○ ○ ○

For the sun-dried tomato pesto, place all the ingredients in a food processor. Pulse until you obtain a semi-smooth mixture where most of the ingredients are fully blended but some sun-dried tomato pieces remain intact. Set aside.

Cook the orzo to al dente according to the package instructions.

Drain and return to the pot. Using a silicone spatula, stir the pesto with the orzo until well coated.

Serve topped with chopped parsley and capers, if desired. Store in the fridge in an airtight container for up to 3 days.

NOTES:

To sneak in an extra serving of veggies, fold two handfuls of baby spinach into the orzo when adding the sun-dried tomato pesto. The heat of the pasta will wilt the spinach.

If you don't have orzo, swap it out for your favorite pasta, including a gluten-free variety!

Quebec Meatless Pie

(NUT/SEED-FREE) (EXTRA PREP)

MAKES: ONE 9½-INCH PIE
PREPARATION: 15 MINUTES
COOKING: 1 HOUR 30 MINUTES
RESTING: 3 HOURS

QUEBEC MEAT PIE, known as *tourtière* in French, is a classic savory pie that is enjoyed mostly during the holiday season and in the spring at sugar shacks across the province. My version features similar techniques and ingredients my mom used in her Christmas savory pie recipe: lots of grated onions, coriander, cumin, and nigella seeds for flavoring. These spices season the "meat" (cooked lentils and bulgur in my version), bringing this dish to life. When I am feeling adventurous (or during the holidays when I spend my days cooking!), I make the crust from scratch. However, if I'm short on time, I often opt for store-bought vegan pie crust. My vegan meat pie is not very traditional, but it's a testimony to the beauty of transforming a traditional dish to one that reflects *you*. Enjoy it on a cool fall day, or for any winter holiday!

CRUST

3 cups (420 g) all-purpose flour

1½ tsp sea salt

1 cup (230 g) cold unsalted vegan butter, cubed

⅓ cup (80 ml) ice water

1 tbsp (15 ml) unsweetened soy milk, for finishing

1 tbsp (15 ml) maple syrup, for finishing

FILLING

½ cup dried brown lentils, rinsed

2¼ cups vegan beef broth or vegetable broth, divided

½ cup bulgur

2 tbsp olive oil

3 onions, grated (see note)

1 large russet or Yukon Gold potato, peeled and grated

PREPARE THE CRUST

In a food processor, mix together the flour and salt. Add the cubed butter and pulse until the butter is incorporated and the mixture has the texture of fine sand. Alternatively, you can use a pastry cutter.

Transfer the mixture to a large bowl and pour in the ice water. Incorporate using your hands, while being careful not to overmix the dough. It should hold together, without being overly tough. Form the dough into a disc. Divide it in two. Cover each piece with plastic wrap and place in the fridge for 1 hour.

PREPARE THE FILLING

Place the lentils along with 1½ cups of broth in a saucepan. Cover and bring to a boil over high heat. Reduce the heat to medium-low and cook until tender but not mushy, about 20 to 25 minutes. There might still be some broth left in the pan; do not discard it. Transfer the lentils along with any remaining broth to a bowl.

In the same pot, bring the remaining ¾ cup of broth to a boil over high heat. Add the bulgur, cover, reduce the heat to medium-low, and cook for 6 to 8 minutes, until the broth has been fully absorbed by the bulgur. Remove from the heat and set aside.

CONTINUED ➤

3 garlic cloves, minced

2½ tsp ground cumin

2 tsp ground coriander

1 tsp nigella seeds or black cumin seeds

¼ tsp chili flakes, plus more to taste

1 packed cup Lacinato or curly kale, cut in bite-sized pieces (see note)

2 tbsp tamari

½ tsp sea salt, plus more to taste

¼ tsp black pepper, plus more to taste

2 tbsp unsweetened soy milk

Heat the olive oil in a large pan set over medium heat. Add the onions and sauté for 5 to 8 minutes, until the onions are translucent and starting to brown.

Stir in the potato, garlic, cumin, coriander, nigella seeds, and chili flakes. Cook, stirring constantly with a wooden spoon, for 1 minute.

Reduce the heat to low and add the lentils (with their broth) to the pan. Stir, then use your wooden spoon to press down on about half of the lentils to mash them slightly—you want about half to remain intact.

Add the kale and tamari, and sprinkle with salt and pepper. Cook until the kale has softened, then add the bulgur and soy milk. Taste and adjust the salt or pepper to your liking. Stir again, then transfer to a large bowl to cool in the fridge for 1 hour 30 minutes.

ASSEMBLE THE PIE

Preheat the oven to 375°F.

Remove the dough discs from the fridge. Dust a clean work surface with flour and roll out both discs into two circles big enough to cover the surface of the pie dish.

Line the bottom of the pie dish with one of the dough circles, gently pressing it into the dish. Scoop in the meat pie filling and spread evenly.

Cover with the second dough disc, pressing the edges together to seal. Cut off the excess dough from around the edges and shape it into decorative pieces to top your pie with, if desired, or freeze for another use. Flute the edges the pie if you would like by pinching the edges of the pie with the index finger and thumb of one hand and pushing in between them with the thumb of the opposite hand.

Poke 3 holes into the center of the pie, to let steam escape during cooking.

In a small bowl, mix together the 1 tablespoon of soy milk and the maple syrup. Brush over the pie.

Bake the pie for 40 to 45 minutes, until the edges and the top are golden brown.

Let cool for at least 30 minutes before slicing. Store leftovers in the fridge in an airtight container for up to 5 days.

Moroccan-Inspired Stuffed Bell Peppers

NUT/SEED-FREE OPTION

EXTRA PREP

MAKES: 4–6 SERVINGS
PREPARATION: 15 MINUTES
COOKING: 1 HOUR 45 MINUTES

ONE OF THE many recipes synonymous with my childhood is stuffed bell peppers. My mom prepared them often when I was growing up, and while I've followed quite a few of her cooking techniques (cooking the bell peppers in a rosé sauce on the stovetop instead of in the oven, for instance), I've made the recipe my own. The flavors are inspired by Moroccan food I've enjoyed in Montreal, the comforting dishes featuring warming spices, dried fruits, and nuts. The stuffing of these bell peppers is a lentil and bulgur mixture flavored with cinnamon, ginger, and turmeric and features dried apricots and pistachios. As the bell peppers simmer and soften, the stuffing absorbs all their juices, resulting in juicy apricots and a luscious filling. Although the pistachios add flavor and texture, if you don't have any on hand or are allergic to them, you can absolutely leave them out or replace them with chopped salted roasted cashews, or leave the nuts out altogether.

STUFFED BELL PEPPERS

- ½ cup dried brown lentils, rinsed (see note)
- 2¼ cups vegan beef broth or vegetable broth, divided
- ½ cup bulgur
- 4 large or 6 medium bell peppers (I use yellow, orange, and red)
- 2 tbsp avocado oil
- 1 large onion, diced
- 1 large carrot, peeled and shredded
- ½ packed cup dried apricots, chopped
- ¼ cup salted roasted pistachios or cashews, chopped
- 4 garlic cloves, minced
- 1¼ tsp sea salt, plus more to taste

PREPARE THE STUFFED BELL PEPPERS

In a small saucepan, place the lentils and 1½ cups of broth. Cover and bring to a boil over high heat. Reduce the heat to medium and cook until the lentils are soft but still have a bite, about 15 minutes. Remove from the heat, drain, and transfer to a large mixing bowl.

Rinse the saucepan and add the remaining ¾ cup of broth to the pan. Cover and bring to a boil over high heat. Stir in the bulgur. Reduce the heat to medium-low, cover, and cook for 6 to 8 minutes or until the broth is absorbed and the bulgur is tender. Remove from the heat and transfer to the bowl with the lentils.

Cut about 1 inch off the top of the bell peppers, reserving them, and remove the placenta and seeds. If your bell peppers cannot stand upright without tipping, also carefully cut off a little bit of the bottom curved edges. Try not to cut any holes in the bell peppers (although, if it happens, no worries, I've accidentally done it at least a dozen times!).

CONTINUED ➤

1¼ tsp ground coriander

¾ tsp ground cinnamon

½ tsp Chinese five-spice powder (see note)

½ tsp Aleppo pepper, plus more to taste

½ tsp ground ginger

½ tsp ground turmeric

½ tsp garlic powder

½ tsp black pepper, plus more to taste

TOMATO BÉCHAMEL

2 tbsp unsalted vegan butter

2 tbsp all-purpose flour

2 cups unsweetened soy milk

1 cup passata (strained tomatoes), from a can or jar

1 tbsp maple syrup

¾ tsp sea salt

¼ tsp black pepper

¼ tsp Aleppo pepper (see note)

¼ tsp Chinese five-spice powder

Chopped fresh parsley, for serving

In a large flat-bottomed sauté pan with a lid that is deep enough for the stuffed bell peppers (with tops on) to sit upright and wide enough to fit them all, heat the avocado oil over medium heat.

Add the onion and carrot. Cook, stirring often with a wooden spoon, until softened and starting to brown, about 8 minutes. Add the apricots, pistachios, garlic, salt, coriander, cinnamon, five-spice powder, Aleppo pepper, ginger, turmeric, garlic powder, and pepper. Stir and cook for 1 minute.

Transfer the vegetable mixture to the bowl with the lentils and bulgur. Stir, taste, and adjust the salt, Aleppo pepper, and pepper to your liking, if desired.

Fill each hollowed-out bell pepper with the filling, being careful not to pack it down. If you have any extra filling, you can reserve it to eat as is.

PREPARE THE TOMATO BÉCHAMEL

Give the sauté pan a quick rinse, then heat the butter in it over medium heat.

Add the flour and cook, stirring constantly with a silicone spatula, until the mixture is light in color. Add the soy milk and increase the heat to medium-high. Continue stirring to incorporate. Bring the mixture to a boil and cook for 2 minutes.

Reduce the heat to medium-low, cook for another 2 minutes or until the mixture is smooth, has thickened, coats the back of your spatula, and has no flour taste.

Pour in the passata and maple syrup. Sprinkle in the salt, pepper, Aleppo pepper, and five-spice powder. Stir until smooth, then turn off the heat.

Place the stuffed bell peppers in the pan with the tomato béchamel and top each with about 1 tablespoon of béchamel. Cover each bell pepper with its cap.

Put the lid on the pan and reduce the heat to low. Cook the peppers for 1 hour. If you notice that the sauce is drying up, test one of the bell peppers. If soft, you can remove the pan from the heat. If not yet cooked through, add 3 tablespoons of water to the pan and stir it through to loosen up the sauce. Turn the heat to your stove's lowest setting and continue cooking until the peppers are done.

Serve with a sprinkling of parsley. Store in the fridge in an airtight container for up to 3 days.

NOTES:

I recommend against using canned lentils in this recipe, because you want the cooked lentils to have a little bit of a bite. Canned lentils tend to be a little too mushy.

If you do not have Aleppo pepper, use chili flakes instead, but halve the amount, unless you'd like this dish to have a good kick.

If you don't have Chinese five-spice powder, you can find an easy recipe online, or garam masala would work in its place.

Caramelized Leek and Onion Risotto

(GLUTEN-FREE) (NUT/SEED-FREE)
(EXTRA PREP)

MAKES: 4 SERVINGS
PREPARATION: 5 MINUTES
COOKING: 45 MINUTES

○

IF YOU HAVE a batch of my Date-Sweetened Leek and Onion Jam (p. 270) and a few extra leeks on hand, this risotto is what you need to make for dinner. Rich, creamy, with a touch of sweetness, and made without any store-bought cheese (unless you want to garnish your risotto with vegan parm!), this main dish is *the* dish when you want to impress a special someone or if you want to treat yourself to an extra special dinner. Do not be intimidated by the cooking process! Take pleasure in the process of pouring the broth into your pan and slowly stirring the rice, helping it turn into a creamy, comforting risotto. Whenever I make risotto, I love to put on some music and pour myself a little glass of wine or kombucha, thereby transforming my cooking into a whole experience.

○ ○

4 cups vegetable or vegan chicken broth

1 tbsp extra virgin olive oil

2 leeks, light green and white parts only, cut in half lengthwise and then into half-moons

2 garlic cloves, minced

1 cup arborio rice

2 tbsp cold unsalted vegan butter

½ cup Date-Sweetened Leek and Onion Jam (p. 270)

2 tbsp nutritional yeast

Black pepper, to taste

Grated vegan parmesan, for serving, optional

Fried onions, for serving, optional

○ ○ ○

In a large saucepan, heat the broth over low heat.

Meanwhile, heat a deep pan over medium-high heat. Add the olive oil and leeks and cook, stirring often with a wooden spoon, until the leeks are softened, slightly translucent, and starting to brown, about 10 to 15 minutes.

Reduce the heat to medium, add the garlic, and cook for 30 seconds. Add the rice and cook for 2 minutes, stirring often.

Pour in ½ cup of warm broth and cook until absorbed, stirring often to help with the absorption.

Repeat the process until you have used up about 3 cups of broth. Taste the rice; you are cooking it until it is just al dente, so if it is still crunchy, add another ½ cup of broth, stir, and cook until absorbed; repeat if needed. I have found that 3½ cups of vegetable broth is usually the sweet spot. Reserve any remaining broth for another use.

Add the cold butter, jam, nutritional yeast, and a generous crack of pepper. Stir until everything is well incorporated.

Remove from the heat and serve topped with grated vegan parmesan and fried onions, if desired.

Lemon Pepper Tempeh

GLUTEN-FREE   NUT/SEED-FREE

MAKES: 4–6 SERVINGS
PREPARATION: 5 MINUTES
COOKING: 25 MINUTES
RESTING: 15 MINUTES

○ ○

2 garlic cloves, grated using a
    Microplane

1 tsp lemon zest

8 tbsp lemon juice

4 tbsp avocado oil, divided

2 tbsp tamari

2 tsp freshly ground black pepper
    (see note)

2 (8½ oz/240 g) packages tempeh,
    cut in 16 triangles

Sliced green onions, for garnish

Cooked rice, for serving

Steamed broccoli, for serving

Cucumber ribbons, for serving,
    optional

○

THIS RECIPE IS FOR those nights when you want to put something together relatively quickly but are also looking to practice a few fun techniques (steaming, marinating, grilling) to infuse flavor into your meal. Steaming the tempeh removes some of its bitterness, and marinating it allows it to slowly infuse with the bright and floral aroma of lemon as well as with the hot and aromatic flavors of black pepper. This tempeh is a wonderful base to a full meal that you can build and adapt to your preferences. I enjoy it most with rice, steamed broccoli, and cucumber ribbons.

○ ○ ○

In a large mixing bowl, prepare the marinade by whisking together the garlic, lemon zest, lemon juice, 2 tablespoons of avocado oil, tamari, and pepper. Set aside.

Set a steamer basket or a foldable steamer in a large saucepan filled with 2 inches of water. Arrange the tempeh in an even layer in the steamer basket. Cover, bring the water to a boil, and then steam over medium-high heat for 15 minutes.

Immediately transfer the tempeh to the bowl with the marinade. Toss using a silicone spatula, cover the bowl with a plate, and let sit for 15 minutes to infuse the tempeh with the marinade's flavors.

Heat the remaining 2 tablespoons of avocado oil in a large pan set over medium heat.

Place the tempeh into the pan, leaving the remaining marinade in the bowl. Cook for 2 to 3 minutes, until brown in color, then flip and cook for another 2 to 3 minutes.

Pour the remaining marinade over the tempeh and stir, using a silicone spatula, to evenly distribute it to every piece.

Remove from the heat and garnish with green onions. Enjoy with rice, broccoli, and cucumber ribbons, if desired. Store in the fridge in an airtight container for up to 2 days.

NOTE:

I strongly suggest using freshly ground pepper in this recipe as opposed to pepper powder. This will result in a much more robust and aromatic pepper flavor that will complement beautifully the brightness of the lemon and fresh garlic.

Coconut-Crusted Tofu with Spicy Mango Salsa

(GLUTEN-FREE) (NUT/SEED-FREE)

MAKES: 4 SERVINGS
PREPARATION: 30 MINUTES
COOKING: 30 MINUTES

WHEN YOU FEEL like traveling to the tropics for some coconut shrimp with a sweet and salty salsa, only to realize that you are unable to escape the cold winter and remember that you are vegan!—your heart and belly will love this recipe! What differentiates my coconut-crusted tofu from others is the flavor within the tofu itself rather than just in the crust. Taking the time to boil the tofu in flavorful broth along with nutritional yeast, garlic powder, and smoked paprika gives it slightly cheesy, smoky, garlicky, and savory qualities. My favorite part about putting this recipe together: carefully coating each individual tofu nugget with the coconut. As I am covering the tofu in coconut, I love envisioning how this step allows the nuggets to be deliciously crispy on the outside, rich, and coconutty.

TOFU

2 cups vegan chicken broth or vegetable broth

¼ cup nutritional yeast

½ tsp garlic powder

½ tsp smoked paprika

1 tsp sea salt

1 (1 lb/454 g) package extra-firm tofu, broken into 1-inch chunks (see note)

½ cup unsweetened soy milk

¼ cup + 1 tbsp brown rice flour

1 tsp chili powder

¼ tsp sea salt

¼ tsp black pepper

1 cup unsweetened shredded coconut

1 tsp dried onion

½ tsp chili flakes

2 tbsp arrowroot powder or cornstarch

Cooking spray

PREPARE THE TOFU

In a medium pot, bring the broth, nutritional yeast, garlic powder, paprika, and salt to a boil over high heat, stirring using a silicone spatula.

Add the tofu pieces and cook, stirring often using your silicone spatula to prevent from sticking, until most of the liquid has evaporated, about 7 to 10 minutes.

Drain, transfer to a large bowl, and let cool for 10 minutes while you prepare the batter and coating.

Prepare the batter by adding the soy milk, brown rice flour, chili powder, salt, and pepper to a bowl. Stir and let sit for 5 minutes to thicken.

In a separate bowl, toss together the coconut, dried onion, and chili flakes.

Line a baking sheet with parchment paper and prepare your station by arranging the 3 bowls in front of you in this order, from left to right: the tofu, the batter in the middle, and the coconut. Place the prepared baking sheet in front of you.

CONTINUED ➤

1 mango, peeled and cut in ½-inch
  cubes

1 cup ½-inch-cubed cucumber

¼ cup finely diced red onion

¼ cup chopped Thai basil
  (see note)

2 tbsp lime juice

¼–½ fresh red chili, finely chopped

¼ tsp sea salt

Sprinkle the arrowroot powder over the tofu and toss to coat using
the silicone spatula.

Use your left hand to drop a piece of tofu in the batter. Coat it with
the batter and give it a shake to remove any excess batter. Still using
your left hand, drop it into the bowl with the coconut.

Use your clean right hand to coat the tofu with coconut, gently
pressing on the coconut to help it stick. Place it on the parchment-
lined baking sheet.

Repeat the process with the remaining tofu.

Preheat the oven to 400°F.

Generously spray each tofu nugget with cooking spray. Bake in
the oven for 15 minutes or until golden. Flip and bake for another
5 minutes.

PREPARE THE SALSA

Toss all the salsa ingredients together in a bowl. If you are sensitive
to heat, start with one-quarter of the chili, seeds included.

Enjoy the tofu with the spicy mango salsa and sushi rice or your
grain of choice.

NOTES:

*Using extra-firm tofu is absolutely key, as the boiling process
will soften the texture of the tofu, and if it is too soft to begin
with, you will end up with super-soggy tofu that will be
impossible to handle.*

If you don't have Thai basil, swap it out with fresh coriander.

Sweet Potato Shiitake Poutine

(CUSTOMIZABLE)
(NUT/SEED-FREE)

MAKES: 4 SERVINGS
PREPARATION: 15 MINUTES
COOKING: 1 HOUR

I AM A Montrealer at heart, so I had to include a poutine recipe in this cookbook. Poutine is a Quebecois dish of fries topped with hot gravy and squeaky cheese. Although traditional poutine has never been my favorite fast-food item, creating elevated versions like this one has awoken my love for this cherished dish. I have spent countless weekends with Sam creating new variations of poutine using all kinds of potatoes, leftover gravy, vegan sausage and ground meat, and various veggies. Poutines are like burgers in that they are an amazing blank canvas on which to express your creativity, practice your culinary skills, and develop your palate. For this recipe, I use sweet potato fries; their sweetness complements all the umami flavors of the decadent gravy that features miso, tamari, and shiitakes. If you have any leftovers, feel free to drizzle it over my Ultimate Mashed Potatoes (p. 104).

○ ○

SWEET POTATO FRIES

4 sweet potatoes, unpeeled and cut
   in ½-inch-thick sticks (see note)

1 tbsp avocado oil

¾ tsp sea salt

½ tsp chili powder

¼ tsp black pepper

MUSHROOM GRAVY

4 cups vegan beef broth or
   vegetable broth

1 cup (40 g) dried whole shiitakes

¼ cup unsalted vegan butter

½ cup finely diced shallots
   (see note)

2 garlic cloves, minced

1 tsp fresh thyme

○ ○ ○

PREPARE THE SWEET POTATO FRIES

Preheat the oven to 400°F. Line a baking sheet with parchment paper or a silicone mat.

Drizzle the sweet potatoes with the avocado oil and sprinkle with the salt, chili powder, and pepper. Toss to coat, then arrange in a single layer on the prepared baking sheet. Bake for 40 to 45 minutes, until tender and browning at the edges. Give the fries a toss halfway through the cooking time.

PREPARE THE MUSHROOM GRAVY

In a small saucepan with the lid on, bring the broth and dried shiitakes to a boil over high heat. Reduce the heat and simmer for 20 minutes, covered.

Remove the shiitakes from the saucepan and set aside. Transfer the broth to a bowl.

CONTINUED ➤

3 tbsp all-purpose flour

1 tbsp whiskey, optional (see note)

2 tsp tamari

2 tsp dark miso paste

½ tsp black pepper

SAUTÉED SHIITAKES

2 tbsp unsalted vegan butter

2 garlic cloves, minced

1 tsp tamari

Black pepper, to taste

TOPPINGS

Vegan feta cheese

Sliced green onions

Return the saucepan to the stove and melt the butter over medium heat. Add the shallots and cook, stirring often using a silicone spatula, for 2 to 3 minutes, until softened.

Add the garlic and thyme, and cook for 1 minute. Sprinkle in the flour and cook for 2 minutes, stirring constantly.

Add the warmed broth, whiskey, tamari, miso, and pepper. Stir, then bring to a boil over high heat. Reduce the heat to medium and cook for 5 minutes, stirring often.

Transfer the mixture to an immersion blender or a regular blender and blend until smooth. Return to the stove and cook over medium heat for 5 more minutes or until thickened. Set aside.

PREPARE THE SAUTÉED SHIITAKES

Thinly slice the rehydrated shiitakes.

Melt the butter in a pan, then add the shiitakes and cook until golden, about 2 minutes.

Sprinkle in the garlic, tamari, and pepper. Stir, then remove the mixture from the heat to prevent burning.

ASSEMBLE THE POUTINE

Divide the sweet potato fries among four individual bowls. Top with crumbled feta, gravy, and sautéed shiitakes. Sprinkle with sliced green onions and serve.

NOTES:

Looking for a more traditional poutine? Use russet or Yukon Gold potatoes instead of sweet potatoes.

Feel free to swap the shallots in the gravy with red onion or yellow onion.

Although the whiskey is optional, I really recommend it! It adds another layer of flavor and makes the ingredients come alive. If you only have bourbon on hand, feel free to use that instead.

Black Beans and Plantain Tacos with Adobo Crema

(CUSTOMIZABLE) (GLUTEN-FREE)
(NUT/SEED-FREE) (EXTRA PREP)

MAKES: 4 SERVINGS
PREPARATION: 15 MINUTES
COOKING: 15 MINUTES

THIS RECIPE IS inspired by a local restaurant in Montreal called Arepera. It is a Venezuelan restaurant that serves the most delicious arepas, which are crispy-on-the-outside corn cakes that can be served plain or stuffed. My two favorite kinds are those filled with black beans and plantains, and those filled with a super-tasty guacamole. Here, I bring both flavors together to create the ultimate taco. When I make this recipe, I love thinking of how each element brings forth a layer of flavor and texture. The sautéed black beans add smokiness and chewiness; the melt-in-your-mouth plantains, sweetness; the avocado mash, brightness and richness; and the silken tofu–based Smoky Adobo Crema (p. 260), creaminess and heat. As you enjoy these tacos, slow down and really appreciate all the flavor profiles you've built into the dish.

1 batch of Pan-Fried Plantains (p. 103), seasoned with sea salt and black pepper

SMOKY BLACK BEANS

1 tbsp avocado oil

1 onion, diced

3 garlic cloves, minced

2 cups black beans, from a can, drained and rinsed

1 tsp chili powder

½ tsp ground coriander

½ tsp smoked paprika

½ tsp sea salt

1 tbsp tomato paste

1 tbsp water

Preheat the oven to 200°F.

Place the fried plantains in the oven to keep warm.

PREPARE THE SMOKY BLACK BEANS

In a large heavy-bottomed pan (such as a cast-iron skillet; it can be the same one you used to make the plantains), heat the avocado oil over medium heat. Add the onion and cook, stirring often with a wooden spoon, until translucent and starting to brown, about 5 minutes.

Sprinkle in the garlic and cook for 30 seconds, then add the black beans, chili powder, coriander, paprika, and salt. Stir, then cook for 1 minute.

Add the tomato paste and water, reduce the heat to medium-low, and cook for 3 to 5 minutes, stirring often. Remove from the heat.

CONTINUED ➤

2 avocadoes

1 tbsp lemon juice

¼ tsp garlic powder

Sea salt and black pepper,
    to taste

OTHER

12 corn tortillas

Smoky Adobo Crema (p. 260)

Fresh coriander, optional

Vegan cheese, optional

PREPARE THE MASHED AVOCADO

Scoop the avocado flesh into a bowl. Mash it with a fork, then season with the lemon juice, garlic powder, salt, and pepper. Stir and set aside.

SERVE THE TACOS

Wrap 4 tortillas in a clean, damp kitchen towel and microwave on high for 45 seconds, warming them up in batches. Alternatively, you can warm them up one by one in a dry, clean pan set over medium heat for 15 to 20 seconds per side.

Serve each taco with a few slices of fried plantains and a spoonful of smoky black beans, mashed avocado, and adobo crema, plus any other toppings of your choice. I love to also add fresh coriander and cheese to my tacos.

Serve hot or store all the ingredients in separate containers in the fridge. The plantain and mashed avocado are best eaten fresh but can be eaten within a day of preparation. The smoky black beans and smoky adobo crema can be stored for up to 3 days. Reheat before enjoying.

NOTE:

Tacos are one of those dishes that is incredibly customizable, so have fun with it! You can incorporate a mango salsa into this dish, or my homemade Bright Chopped Salsa (p. 266). Caramelized onions or my Pickled Onions (p. 267) are always an option too.

Sesame Ginger Glazed Shiitakes with Sticky Rice

(GLUTEN-FREE) (NUT/SEED-FREE)

MAKES: 4 SERVINGS
PREPARATION: 10 MINUTES
COOKING: 30 MINUTES

○ ○

STICKY RICE

2 cups water

1 cup Calrose rice

1 tsp sea salt

2 tbsp rice vinegar

1 tbsp + 1½ tsp organic cane sugar

SHIITAKES

3 tbsp tamari

4 garlic cloves

1 thumb-sized piece of ginger

1 tbsp sesame oil

1 tbsp maple syrup

3 tbsp cornstarch

5 cups (250 g) fresh shiitakes

2 tbsp avocado oil

Sliced green onion, for garnish

Sesame seeds, for garnish

Cucumbers, cut into sticks, for serving

○ HAVING SPENT SO many hours in the kitchen, I have come to learn that sometimes you can create little luxuries from a simple process and only a few ingredients. This recipe is just that: it is straightforward to put together, but will make you feel like you're dining out at a trendy restaurant. Slightly smoky, savory, and packed with umami flavors, these sesame ginger glazed shiitakes are wonderful when paired with sticky rice and fresh veggies. When it comes together, this bowl reminds me of a fancy sushi bowl, minus the seaweed. When I've had a long week and Friday night comes around, instead of ordering out, I run to the store, buy some shiitakes, and treat myself to this flavor-packed dinner. I hope you will too!

○ ○ ○

PREPARE THE RICE

Pour the water into a saucepan, cover, and bring to a boil.

Rinse the rice in a mesh strainer until the water runs clear.

Add the rice to the boiling water, along with the salt. Stir, reduce the heat to low, and cook, covered, for 18 minutes.

Remove from the heat and let sit for 5 minutes.

Meanwhile, in a small bowl, stir together the rice vinegar and sugar until the sugar is dissolved.

Pour the mixture over the rice and stir to distribute evenly. Let it sit, uncovered, for at least 10 minutes, while you prepare the shiitakes.

PREPARE THE SHIITAKES

Place the tamari in a small bowl. Using a Microplane, grate the garlic and ginger into the bowl. Add the sesame oil and maple syrup, and stir using a silicone spatula. Set the sauce aside.

Pour the cornstarch into a large mixing bowl. Set aside.

CONTINUED ➤

Place the shiitakes in a mesh strainer and rinse them under water for 5 seconds—you only want to get them lightly wet, not soaked.

Toss the shiitakes with the cornstarch to coat. Set aside.

Heat the avocado oil in a large nonstick pan set over medium-high heat. Add the shiitakes, leaving any excess cornstarch in the bowl.

Sauté the mushrooms, tossing them often with a silicone spatula, until a thin, golden-brown crispy crust forms, about 7 to 10 minutes.

Pour the sauce over the mushrooms and cook for 30 seconds, stirring constantly, just until the mushrooms are coated.

Garnish with green onions and sesame seeds. Serve alongside the sticky rice and cucumber.

Dumpling Dough

(NUT/SEED-FREE) (EXTRA PREP)

MAKES: 40–48 DUMPLINGS
PREPARATION: 1 HOUR
RESTING: 30 MINUTES

○

THIS IS THE base dough for my Potato-Onion Varenyky (p. 187) and Lentil Pelmeni (p. 189). Although many of the traditional Russian and Ukrainian recipes for these dumplings use eggs in the dough, this one is completely vegan. My key to a smooth pasta dough is to use warm water and be very patient when preparing it. Any recipe that requires kneading or rolling or getting in there in one way or the other with your hands to bring a dish to life is an opportunity to slow down and connect to your food. I particularly love making this recipe with a loved one and including them in the process of filling and assembling the dumplings. If you want to use this dough for both varenyky and pelmeni, simply halve the measurements for both fillings when you make them.

○ ○

2 cups (280 g) all-purpose flour, plus more as needed

½ tsp sea salt

1 tbsp (15 ml) canola oil

½ cup (125 ml) warm water (about 130°F), plus more as needed

○ ○ ○

In a large bowl, stir together the flour and salt with a fork. Drizzle in the canola oil.

Incorporate the warm water 1 tablespoon at a time, stirring with a fork between each addition until the dough starts to come together.

Knead the dough in the bowl for about 5 minutes—the dough will be very dense. If the dough is really not coming together, add more warm water, 1 teaspoon at a time, and kneading your dough for a good minute between each addition. If your dough becomes too sticky, add flour, 1 teaspoon at a time, again kneading between additions. Using your hands, form the dough into a ball.

Transfer the dough to a clean work surface. Lightly oil your hands with canola oil and knead the dough for 5 more minutes or until the dough comes together and is smooth and softer.

Divide the dough into 4 equal pieces, and set 3 of them on a plate, covered with a damp, clean kitchen towel to prevent them from drying out.

Knead the fourth piece for 3 minutes, then place it on the plate. Repeat the process with the remaining 3 pieces. If the dough is sticking to your work surface, very lightly flour the work surface.

Let the dough pieces rest, covered with the damp towel, at room temperature for 30 minutes.

Very lightly flour your work surface. Roll a piece of dough into a circle 10 inches in diameter and 1 mm thick. If you find that your dough is difficult to spread, lightly brush it with water, flip it on its damp side, then roll again.

Using a 3-inch round cookie cutter (or the sharp edge of a mason jar lid), cut 10 to 12 circles out of your dough.

Take one of the circles and roll it out to 3½ inches in diameter. Repeat the process with the remaining pieces. Place on a plate or baking sheet and cover with a damp, clean kitchen towel to prevent from drying out (it's okay to stack up some of the circles, they should be dry enough not to stick together). Repeat the process with the remaining 3 pieces of dough. You should have between 40 and 48 circles of dough in the end. Use immediately.

Potato-Onion Varenyky

(NUT/SEED-FREE) (EXTRA PREP)

MAKES: 4 SERVINGS
PREPARATION: 30 MINUTES
COOKING: 35 MINUTES
RESTING: 30 MINUTES

○ VARENYKY ARE TRADITIONAL Ukrainian dumplings, the Ukrainian version of Polish pierogi. They are most commonly filled with potato. My version is inspired by the kind my mom made for the family when I was growing up. The filling consisted not only of mashed potatoes but also slowly browned onions. The step of cooking down the onions for a light caramelization is what makes this filling divine, in my opinion. Take your time with it, noticing how the onions go from crisp and bright to soft, buttery, and golden brown. Once your filling is ready, assemble the varenyky one at a time, gently placing the filling in the middle of each dough circle, folding over the dough, and sealing the edges carefully. I can promise you that all the time and love spent making these will be felt within your first bite!

○○

2 Yukon Gold potatoes, peeled and cubed

2 garlic cloves

2 bay leaves, divided

1 tsp sea salt, plus more to taste

3 tbsp unsalted vegan butter, plus more for coating

2 onions, diced

Black pepper, to taste

1 batch Dumpling Dough (p. 184), cut into 40–48 circles

Vegan sour cream, for serving, optional

○○○

PREPARE THE FILLING

In a medium pot, place the potatoes, garlic cloves, 1 bay leaf, and salt. Cover with water and the lid. Turn the heat to high and bring to a boil. Then reduce the heat to medium and cook until the potatoes are very soft, 12 to 15 minutes.

Drain, remove the bay leaf, and mash the mixture until smooth. Set aside.

In a large sauté pan set over medium heat, melt the butter. Add the onions and cook, stirring often with a wooden spoon, until they are just starting to change color. Reduce the heat to low and cook until soft and golden brown, about 10 to 15 minutes. You do not want the onions to be deep brown and crispy, but rather golden brown and soft.

Season with salt and pepper. Add half of the onions to the mashed potatoes, stir, taste, and adjust the levels of salt and pepper to your liking.

Let cool completely before using as a filling.

CONTINUED ➤

ASSEMBLE THE VARENYKY

On a clean work surface, line up 6 dough circles, keeping the rest covered with a damp, clean kitchen towel. Place a cup of water and a plate in front of you.

Scoop about 2 teaspoons of filling onto the center of each dough circle.

Dip a fingertip in the water and then gently brush the water onto the outer edge of the dough.

Fold the dough over to encase the filling, and use your fingertips to pinch the edges together to seal, starting at one end of the dumpling and making your way to the other. Then fold the edges over or press with the tines of a fork to create a pattern.

Place on the plate and continue to fill the remaining dough circles.

Bring a large pot of salted water to a boil with the remaining bay leaf.

Carefully drop the varenyky into the boiling water. Stir to prevent them from sticking to the bottom of the pot. Cook for about 3 minutes, or until they float to the surface.

Transfer the cooked varenyky to a large bowl, using a slotted spoon. Add the remaining caramelized onions, tossing to coat. Add some butter to prevent sticking, if desired.

Season with a crack of pepper, then enjoy the varenyky on their own or with vegan sour cream. Store in the fridge in an airtight container for up to 2 days.

NOTE:

You can add a kick to the filling by seasoning it with smoked paprika, chili flakes, or cayenne pepper.

Lentil Pelmeni

(NUT/SEED-FREE)   (EXTRA PREP)

MAKES: 4 SERVINGS
PREPARATION: 30 MINUTES
COOKING: 25 MINUTES
RESTING: 1 HOUR

○ ○

½ cup dried brown lentils
   (do not rinse)

½ cup water

1½ tbsp olive oil, plus more
   for coating

1 onion, finely diced

2 garlic cloves, grated using
   a Microplane

½ tsp sea salt

½ tsp smoked paprika

½ tsp ground coriander

Pinch of black pepper, plus
   more for garnish

⅓ cup cooked white rice (see note)

1 batch Dumpling Dough (p. 184),
   cut into 40–48 circles

1 bay leaf

○

WHILE VARENYKY (P. 189) are stuffed with a potato filling, traditional pelmeni typically have a meaty filling. To replace the pork or beef in the traditional recipe, I use brown lentils, which gives the filling a denser texture. By incorporating lots of onions, a variety of spices, and cooked white rice, my version not only packs a flavor punch but is also complex in texture. As you put these pelmeni together, you will have to lean into trusting the recipe and the process because, unlike with my varenyky filling, this filling comes together only once the pelmeni is boiled, due to the raw lentils. But let me reassure you, the result is a satisfying main dish that can be enjoyed on its own or with a green salad as a side for extra freshness.

○ ○ ○

PREPARE THE FILLING

Blend the lentils in a high-speed blender or a food processor until you obtain a fine sand-like texture.

Transfer to a bowl and cover with the water. Stir, then let sit for 30 minutes to absorb the water.

Heat the olive oil in a large sauté pan set over medium heat. Add the onion and cook, stirring often with a wooden spoon, until it is just starting to change color.

Reduce the heat to low and continue to cook, stirring often, until soft and golden brown, about 10 to 15 minutes. You do not want them to be deep brown and crispy, but rather golden brown and soft.

Stir in the garlic and cook for 1 minute. Season with the salt, paprika, coriander, and pepper. Stir to combine.

Add the lentils and cook for 5 minutes, stirring often.

Fold in the cooked rice and let cool completely.

CONTINUED ➤

Olive oil or unsalted vegan butter,
for coating

Vegan sour cream, for serving,
optional

Chopped chives, for garnish,
optional

ASSEMBLE THE PELMENI

On a clean work surface, line up 6 dough circles, keeping the rest covered with a damp, clean kitchen towel. Place a cup of water and a plate in front of you.

Scoop 2 teaspoons of filling onto the center of each circle.

Dip a fingertip in the water and then gently brush the water on the outer edge of the dough.

Fold the dough over to encase the filling, and use your fingertips to pinch the edges together to seal, starting at one end of the dumpling and making your way to the other. Then fold the edges over or press with the tines of a fork to create a pattern.

Place on the plate and continue to fill the remaining dough circles.

Bring a large pot of salted water to a boil with the remaining bay leaf.

Carefully drop the pelmeni into the boiling water. Stir to prevent them from sticking to the bottom of the pot. Cook for about 3 minutes, or until they float to the surface.

Transfer the cooked pelmeni to a large bowl, using a slotted spoon. Coat with olive oil and season with a crack of pepper.

Enjoy the pelmeni on their own or with vegan sour cream and chives. Store in the fridge in an airtight container for up to 2 days.

NOTE:

Feel free to use basmati or jasmine rice.

NOTES:

To add a little extra luxury to your sauce, replace two of the garlic cloves with two black garlic cloves. Peel them and add them whole at the same time as the grated garlic, then press down on the cloves in the pan using your spatula to break them down.

I suggest opting for a white wine that is not too acidic, or it will make your sauce too acidic.

Kalamata Olives Rosé Linguini

(GLUTEN-FREE OPTION)

(NUT/SEED-FREE)

MAKES: 4 SERVINGS
PREPARATION: 10 MINUTES
COOKING: 20 MINUTES

IF THERE IS one non-vegan food that I miss, it is seafood. I used to adore calamari, crab, oysters, clams, salmon, and shrimp. Although it can be quite hard to fully replicate the flavor of seafood in your kitchen, I've come close with this linguini dish. It is a dish that feels very luxurious, like one you would make if you wanted to treat yourself or a loved one. The mix of white wine with buttery shallots, pungent garlic, and salty, briny Kalamata olives all cooked together in a simple rosé sauce and paired with linguini truly reminds me of a dish that could be served on a terrace somewhere in Italy. Pair it with a glass of your favorite white wine, kombucha, or fresh lemony water to instantly feel transported to the seaside.

1 (12 oz/340 g) package linguini

3 tbsp olive oil, divided

2 shallots, finely diced

6 garlic cloves, grated using a Microplane (see note)

Sea salt and black pepper, to taste

½ cup good-quality white wine (I like sauvignon blanc; see note)

1 tbsp unsalted vegan butter

1 tbsp all-purpose flour

1 cup unsweetened soy milk

1 cup passata (strained tomatoes) or tomato coulis

2 tbsp tomato paste

½ cup Kalamata olives, pitted and finely chopped

Vegan parmesan shavings, for serving

Cook the linguine according to the package instructions. Drain and toss in 1 tablespoon of olive oil.

Heat the remaining 2 tablespoons of olive oil in a large pan set over medium heat. Add the shallots and cook until translucent, about 4 minutes, stirring often with a silicone spatula. Sprinkle in the garlic and season with a generous pinch of salt and pepper or to taste. Stir and cook for 1 to 2 minutes, until the garlic begins to brown.

Pour in the white wine and stir with your spatula to detach any of the shallots or garlic pieces that have stuck to the pan. Cook until the wine has been mostly absorbed, about 5 minutes.

Add the butter and sprinkle in the flour. Cook for 1 minute, stirring often, making sure the butter is completely melted.

Pour in the soy milk and cook until the sauce thickens enough to coat the back of a spoon. Add the passata and tomato paste. Stir to fully incorporate. Gently stir in the olives. Taste and season with more salt and pepper to your liking.

Transfer the cooked linguine to the pan, stirring to coat with the sauce. Distribute the pasta among individual bowls and enjoy with a generous crack of pepper and vegan parmesan shavings. Store in the fridge in an airtight container for up to 2 days.

Butter Chicken-Style Lentils

(GLUTEN-FREE) (NUT/SEED-FREE)

MAKES: 4–6 SERVINGS
PREPARATION: 5 MINUTES
COOKING: 30 MINUTES

○ ○

1½ cups dried red lentils

1 tbsp avocado oil

1 large onion, diced

3 garlic cloves, grated using a
    Microplane

1 tbsp grated ginger, grated using
    a Microplane

1 tbsp + 1 tsp garam masala

1 tbsp + 1 tsp curry powder

1 tsp ground coriander

Cayenne pepper, to taste

¾ tsp sea salt

1 cup diced or crushed tomatoes,
    from a can

2 tbsp tomato paste

1 (13½ oz/400 ml) can full-fat
    coconut milk

1¼ cups water

½ cup dried cranberries (see note)

Basmati rice, for serving

Naan, for serving

Chopped chives, for garnish

Chili flakes, for garnish

○

BECAUSE I LOVE the rich and complex flavors of butter chicken, I wanted to create a recipe inspired by that divine dish that holds many memories. I had to break down all the elements of butter chicken and spend some time testing variations in order to find the perfect balance of spices, sweetness, acidity, and richness. I'm so happy with the final result! Although my version is closer to a dal than actual butter chicken texture-wise (because I used lentils and not tofu or seitan), many spices and flavors that are typically found in butter chicken are present in this dish too. My version, though, has an unusual little twist: tangy and sweet dried cranberries.

○ ○ ○

Rinse the lentils in a mesh strainer. Set aside.

Heat a large saucepan over medium heat. Add the avocado oil and onion and cook, stirring often, until the onion starts to caramelize, about 8 minutes.

Stir in the garlic, ginger, garam masala, curry powder, coriander, cayenne, and salt, then cook for 1 minute.

Add the lentils, tomatoes, tomato paste, coconut milk, water, and dried cranberries. Stir, then bring to a boil over high heat.

Reduce the heat to low and cook, covered, for 15 minutes, stirring every once in a while.

Garnish with chives and chili flakes. Enjoy alongside basmati rice and naan. Store in the fridge in an airtight container for up to 5 days.

NOTE:

If you don't have cranberries, swap them out with raisins or chopped prunes.

Savory Stuffed Crepes

(NUT/SEED-FREE) (EXTRA PREP)

MAKES: 4–6 SERVINGS
PREPARATION: 10 MINUTES
COOKING: 20 MINUTES

WHEN MY FAMILY immigrated to Canada and my mom became in charge of all the cooking, she made some North American dishes, but she also recreated some of the Russian and Ukrainian dishes she had grown up eating, including this family favorite. Filling them with lots of onion, ground beef, and rice, my mom usually reserved these crepes for weekend dinners or special occasions, as they require a little extra prep and love to put together. I have always loved the subtle flavors of her crepes, and I wanted to recreate something similar here. My Mom's Classic Crepes (p. 35) are beautifully supple, making them super easy to roll. They also have a touch of sweetness, which pairs wonderfully with TVP Rice and Beans (p. 198). To enjoy these crepes as my family did, serve them with vegan sour cream. It brings a delightful creaminess and tanginess to this Eastern European classic.

1½ tsp vegan butter, melted

1 batch of My Mom's Classic Crepes (p. 35), made without vanilla extract and cooled

1 batch of TVP Rice and Beans (p. 198), cooled

Chopped chives, for garnish

Vegan sour cream, for serving

Preheat the oven to 350°F. Lightly brush a baking dish with the butter.

Place a crepe on a plate. Scoop ¼ cup of TVP Rice and Beans onto the bottom one-third of the crepe, leaving a 2-inch border below and on each side of the mixture.

Fold the right and left sides of the crepe inward, then fold up the bottom part of the crepe. Tightly roll the crepe, starting at the end with the rice mixture. Place in the prepared baking dish, seam side down. Repeat the process with the remaining crepes and rice mixture.

Brush the crepes with the remaining butter (you won't have much left, and that's okay!).

Cover the baking dish tightly with foil. Bake for 20 minutes or until warm through.

Garnish with chives, and serve with vegan sour cream. Store in the fridge in an airtight container for up to 3 days.

TVP Rice and Beans

(GLUTEN-FREE) (NUT/SEED-FREE)

MAKES: 4–6 SERVINGS
PREPARATION: 10 MINUTES
COOKING: 10 MINUTES

IF YOU ARE looking for a tasty dish that is simple to make and packed with protein, look no further. This dish uses TVP, also known as textured vegetable protein. Not only is TVP really high in protein, it is also a versatile ingredient that adds lots of texture to any dish. For these rice and beans, I simply rehydrate it in a vegan broth for 10 minutes to turn it into a chewy mixture that resembles ground meat. It's then cooked with onion, garlic, black beans, and spices before being added to rice to create a mixture that can be eaten on its own for lunch and dinner or as a side dish. If you want to spend extra time with this dish, transform it into Savory Stuffed Crepes (p 197).

○○

1 cup TVP (I like Bob's Red Mill)

½ cup hot vegetable broth

1 tbsp avocado oil

1 cup diced onion

1 cup black beans, from a can, drained and rinsed

2 garlic cloves, minced

2 tbsp tamari

1 tsp balsamic vinegar

½ tsp Chinese five-spice powder

¼ tsp black pepper

Pinch of cayenne pepper

1 cup cooled cooked white or brown rice (see note)

Sea salt, to taste

○○○

Place the TVP in a bowl and pour the hot vegetable broth overtop. Stir and let sit for 10 minutes to rehydrate.

Heat a large pan over medium heat. Add the avocado oil and onion and cook, stirring often, until the onion is translucent and starting to caramelize, about 6 minutes.

Add the rehydrated TVP, black beans, garlic, tamari, balsamic vinegar, five-spice powder, pepper, and a pinch of cayenne, and cook for 2 minutes, stirring often to evenly distribute all the spices and ingredients. Add the cooked rice and stir to distribute evenly. Heat for 2 minutes. Taste and adjust the salt and heat levels to your liking.

Remove from the heat and enjoy. Store in the fridge in an airtight container for up to 5 days.

NOTE:

When making this as a side dish or for my Savory Stuffed Crepes (p. 197), I find that long grain white rice works best to keep it light. If you're eating this as a main dish, brown rice will work well.

Smoky Split Pea Soup

(CUSTOMIZABLE) (GLUTEN-FREE)
(NUT/SEED-FREE) (EXTRA PREP)

MAKES: 4 SERVINGS
PREPARATION: 10 MINUTES
COOKING: 45 MINUTES
RESTING: 8 HOURS

○ ONE OF MY MOM'S signature soups is a rich, made-with-love smoky split pea soup that features chewy pieces of bacon. I wanted to recreate this recipe for this cookbook, so I turned to her almost entirely for this recipe. One of the first things she told me as we prepared this soup on a cold winter evening was that rushing the cooking would rob this soup of all its flavor. Taking the time to brown the onion, carrot, bell pepper, and cauliflower allows for their richness and depth to come to life. Together, we learned that most groceries carry imitation bacon bits that are 100% vegan, made with soy protein but with that traditional smoky and salty bacon flavor. When soaked in the broth, they release their flavor, making for a scrumptious, comforting winter soup.

○ ○

1 cup dried green split peas

2 tbsp canola oil

1 onion, finely diced

1 carrot, peeled and finely diced

1 red or orange bell pepper, cored and finely diced

1 cup small cauliflower florets (see note)

3 tbsp imitation bacon bits

½ tsp garlic powder

⅛ tsp chili flakes

Black pepper, to taste

4 cups water, plus more for soaking

1 bay leaf

1 tsp sea salt

½ tsp whole mixed peppercorns

1 small Yukon Gold potato, peeled and finely diced

1 tbsp unsalted vegan butter, optional

No-Knead Overnight Dutch Oven Bread (p. 63), optional

○ ○ ○

In a large bowl, cover the split peas with water. Soak for 8 to 12 hours.

Heat the canola oil in a large sauté pan set over medium heat. Add the onion, carrot, bell pepper, cauliflower florets, imitation bacon bits, garlic powder, chili flakes, and pepper. Cook, stirring often, for 10 to 15 minutes, until everything has softened and browned. Remove from the heat. Set aside.

Drain the split peas, rinse well, and transfer to a large pot. Cover with the water and add the bay leaf, salt, and peppercorns. Bring to a boil over high heat, covered. Reduce the heat to low and keep cooking, covered, for 8 to 10 minutes.

Add the potato to the split peas and increase the heat to bring the mixture to a boil. Then reduce the heat to low and cook, covered, for 8 to 10 more minutes, until the potato is cooked through.

Add the vegetable mixture and also the butter, if desired for extra richness. Stir, cover, and cook over low heat for 3 minutes.

Taste and adjust the seasonings to your liking.

Enjoy alongside a slice of bread. Store in the fridge in an airtight container for up to 5 days.

NOTE:

You can swap the cauliflower with an equal amount of small broccoli florets or cubed button mushrooms.

Sweet Pea and Dill Soup

(GLUTEN-FREE)

MAKES: 4–6 SERVINGS
PREPARATION: 5 MINUTES
COOKING: 15 MINUTES

○

THE VERY FIRST TIME I tried sweet green pea soup was when my mother-in-law made her famous rendition for the holidays. At first glance, I was shocked by the soup's vibrant color. At first taste, I fell in love. I was amazed by how light, velvety, sweet, and savory it was. Years later, this soup is still engrained in my mind as one of the best soups I have ever had—so I *had* to include a version in my cookbook. Mine features the same sweet green peas and vegetable broth base as my mother-in-law's, but with a few additions. Fresh dill adds herbaceous notes, while the hemp hearts bring forth a little nuttiness and some extra proteins. If you are feeling extra fancy and have microgreens on hand, sprinkle them onto this soup, as they make the most beautiful garnish!

○ ○

1 tbsp extra virgin olive oil, plus more for garnish

1 onion, diced

4 cups vegetable broth

5 cups frozen green peas

½ cup loosely packed fresh dill, plus more for garnish

6 tbsp hemp hearts

2 tbsp nutritional yeast

½ tsp black pepper, plus more to taste

Sea salt, to taste

Microgreens, for garnish, optional

○ ○ ○

Heat a large saucepan over medium heat. Add the olive oil and onion. Cook, stirring often with a silicone spatula, until the onion is translucent and starting to brown, about 6 minutes.

Pour in the vegetable broth, increase the heat to high, and bring to a boil.

Add the frozen peas, stir, then cook for 2 minutes or until the peas have thawed.

Transfer the mixture to a high-speed blender. Add the dill, hemp hearts, nutritional yeast, and pepper. Blend until smooth.

Taste and adjust the seasonings to your liking.

If necessary, return the mixture to the saucepan and heat over medium-low heat until warmed through.

Garnish with a drizzle of olive oil, fresh dill, pepper, and microgreens, and serve. Store in the fridge in an airtight container for up to 3 days.

Sweet Potato and Corn Bisque

(GLUTEN-FREE) (NUT/SEED-FREE)

MAKES: 4–6 SERVINGS
PREPARATION: 10 MINUTES
COOKING: 40 MINUTES
RESTING: 5 MINUTES

VERY OFTEN, my recipe ideas arise from random cravings. One afternoon, I could not stop thinking about seafood soup. Although I had actually never eaten a seafood bisque or chowder in my life, I decided to experiment with ways to bring forth the idea of seafood with vegan ingredients and found that Old Bay Seasoning, together with a bit of nori and sweet potatoes, somewhat surprisingly gave me the exact result I was looking for. This soup has delightful notes of sweetness, umami, and cream. Its base is mostly smooth, with texture added from whole corn kernels, similar to traditional chowder.

○ ○

1 tbsp avocado oil

3 shallots, diced

2 sweet potatoes, peeled and cut in ½-inch cubes

1 Yukon Gold or russet potato, peeled and cut in ½-inch cubes

½ red or orange bell pepper, diced

1 (12 oz/341 ml) can corn kernels, drained

3 garlic cloves, minced

2 tsp Old Bay Seasoning

1 tsp dried thyme

¼ tsp smoked paprika

1 tbsp tomato paste

3 cups vegetable broth, plus more as needed

1 bay leaf

½ sheet nori, broken into ½-inch pieces

1 cup soy cream (such as Belsoy)

1 tbsp lime juice

¼ tsp black pepper, plus more for garnish

Chives, for garnish

○ ○ ○

Heat the avocado oil in a large pot set over medium heat. Add the shallots and cook, stirring often with a wooden spoon, for 3 to 4 minutes, until translucent.

Add the sweet potatoes, potato, and bell pepper and cook, stirring often, for 8 to 10 minutes, until the bell pepper has softened.

Measure out ¼ cup of corn and reserve for garnish.

Sprinkle the garlic, Old Bay Seasoning, thyme, and paprika over the sautéed vegetables. Add ¾ cup of corn and the tomato paste. Sauté for 2 minutes.

Pour in the vegetable broth. Add the bay leaf and nori. Increase the heat to high and bring the mixture to a boil. Once boiling, reduce the heat to low and cook, covered, for 15 to 20 minutes, until the potatoes are tender.

Remove from the heat and let cool for 5 minutes. Measure out 2 tablespoons of soy cream and reserve for garnish.

Remove the bay leaf from the soup, then transfer the soup to a blender along with the remaining soy cream, lime juice, and pepper. Blend until smooth.

Return the soup to the pot and stir in the remaining corn kernels from the can. If the soup has cooled down too much, warm it up for a few minutes before serving. If the texture is too thick, you can stir in a little extra vegetable broth.

Serve garnished with the reserved corn, soy cream, chives, and a crack of pepper. Store leftovers in the fridge in an airtight container for up to 3 days.

Desserts are where my love for cooking truly began. With the very first decadent chocolate cake I served my family, I tapped into a passion.

The fact that many of us end our meals with a sweet dish implies something profound about this course. In my family, dessert is always paired with a cup of tea or coffee, which slows down the tasting process, inspiring us all to savor every sip and sweet bite. I view this ritual as a celebration of food, of the hands that prepared it, and of the meal, now closing.

In this light, as you make the desserts in this chapter, infuse a little luxury into your process. Take extra time melting the chocolate, poaching the pears, or forming the cookies. This love will show in your dessert, closing off your meal with grace and sweetness.

Delectable Desserts

Piña Colada Cakes

(NUT/SEED-FREE)

MAKES: 8 MINI CAKES
PREPARATION: 10 MINUTES
COOKING: 45 MINUTES

THESE MINI UPSIDE-DOWN CAKES are everything I absolutely love about tropical fruits and flavors. The sponge is made of cake flour, which yields a delightfully light texture. However, the true stars of this dessert are the pineapple slices and its luscious caramel. The pineapple's very distinct sweet and slightly sour flavor is brought to life by the silky caramel and the subtle toasted aroma of the brown rum. This recipe requires you to be fully present when making it—and *especially* during the making of the caramel. Try not to walk away from the stove or multitask; instead, notice how the sugar goes from fully granulated to melted and finally to golden brown. I am hoping that, with this dessert, you feel transported to a tropical destination, even if you are eating it in the middle of the winter!

⅓ cup (67 g) + ½ cup (100 g) organic cane sugar, divided

1 heaping cup (7 oz/200 g) fresh pineapple, peeled, cored, and cut in ¼-inch triangles (see note)

1 tbsp (15 g) unsalted vegan butter

1 tbsp (15 ml) brown rum

1½ cups (180 g) cake flour

1 tsp baking powder

¾ tsp baking soda

¼ tsp sea salt

¾ cup (185 ml) unsweetened coconut beverage, from a carton (see note)

1 tsp coconut extract, optional

Coconut whipped cream, for serving, optional

Toasted unsweetened shredded coconut, for serving, optional (see note)

Grease 8 cups of a muffin pan with cooking spray or melted virgin coconut oil.

Evenly sprinkle ⅓ cup (67 g) of sugar in a flat-bottomed saucepan and heat over medium-low heat. Do not stir.

Once most of the sugar has melted, with only a few dry spots remaining, about 10 minutes into the cooking process, stir using a silicone spatula.

Cook for another 1 to 3 minutes, until the sugar has fully melted and its color is somewhere between gold and light amber. Add the pineapple pieces, butter, and rum.

Cook, stirring constantly, for 10 minutes or until the sugar that has seized up is fully dissolved and the pineapple slices are softened. I find that using a silicone spatula to press the hardened sugar onto the saucepan helps melt it faster.

Divide the pineapple and syrup among the 8 prepared muffin cups. Set aside.

Preheat the oven to 350°F.

In a large bowl, sift together the flour, remaining ½ cup (100 g) of sugar, baking powder, baking soda, and salt. Stir to combine.

CONTINUED ➤

Add the coconut beverage and coconut extract, if using, and whisk until incorporated and no streaks of flour remain. Be careful not to overmix.

Divide the batter between the 8 muffin cups—I find that about 2 heaping tablespoons per cup is enough to fill them.

Bake in the oven for 14 to 18 minutes, until a toothpick inserted into the center comes out clean and the mini cakes are golden at the edges.

Remove from the oven and let cool in the pan for 5 minutes.

Line a baking sheet with parchment paper and invert the cakes onto it.

Enjoy these mini cakes warm on their own or with a dollop of coconut whipped cream and garnished with toasted shredded coconut, if desired.

Store in the fridge in an airtight container for up to 3 days. Warm up in the microwave on medium power for 15 seconds before enjoying again.

NOTES:

Choose a pineapple that is not too ripe, to avoid the cakes being overly sweet.

If you don't have coconut beverage, replace it with your unsweetened nondairy milk of choice (soy, oat, cashew, etc.), but make sure to then use coconut extract in the recipe.

Toast your shredded coconut in a dry pan set on medium-low heat, until golden brown, stirring often using a wooden spoon.

Chocolate Kolbasa

(CUSTOMIZABLE)

(GLUTEN-FREE OPTION)

(NUT/SEED-FREE) (EXTRA PREP)

MAKES: TWO 8-INCH LOGS
PREPARATION: 15 MINUTES
COOKING: 10 MINUTES
RESTING: 3 HOURS

○

CHOCOLATE KOLBASA (SALAMI), popular in both Russia and Italy, is a mixture of crushed cookies, dried fruits, melted chocolate, butter, and nuts, all rolled up into a log. My version does not contain nuts, but the amazing thing about this recipe (apart from its flavor!) is how customizable it is. You can really have fun playing around with its fillings to create a dessert that caters to *you* by mixing in your favorite cookies, for example, or even by adding some festive liqueur to the mix. When making this version, I thought hard about what combination of rich, creamy chocolate, crunchy cookies, and dried fruits, with their slight tanginess and chewiness, would make a dessert that is truly unique and full of texture. I encourage you to do the same when you are experimenting with your own versions.

○ ○

7 oz (200 g) store-bought crunchy vegan cookies (such as Biscoff, vegan graham, or digestive)

1 heaping cup (150 g) chopped dark chocolate (I use 85%)

⅓ cup (75 g) unsalted vegan butter

⅓ cup (80 ml) unsweetened soy milk (see note)

½ cup (50 g) dried cranberries, coarsely chopped

½ cup (50 g) raisins, coarsely chopped

½ tsp sea salt

2 tbsp (15 g) powdered sugar

○ ○ ○

Cut 2 pieces of parchment paper into 12-inch squares, and have 4 rubber elastics or twine at the ready.

In a food processor (see note), pulse the cookies until about half of them are ground and the other half remains in chunks. If some chunks are significantly bigger than others (more than 1 inch wide), break them up with your hands. Set aside.

Place the dark chocolate, butter, and soy milk in a large, heatproof mixing bowl. Fill a medium saucepan (big enough to hold your bowl without having it touch the bottom) with 1 inch of water. Set the bowl with the chocolate mixture on top of the saucepan and heat on medium-low heat to melt the chocolate and butter.

Stir the mixture with a silicone spatula every minute or so until the chocolate and butter are fully melted and combined.

Fold in the cookie crumbs and chunks, cranberries, raisins, and salt until all the ingredients are coated with the chocolate mixture.

Transfer half of the mixture to a prepared parchment paper square, placing it on the bottom third of the parchment, leaving a 2-inch border below and on each side.

CONTINUED ➤

Fold the parchment over the mixture and roll it into a tight log with your hands. Tie both ends of the parchment with the elastics or twine.

Repeat the process with the remaining mixture. Place both logs in the fridge for at least 3 hours to set.

Before serving, unroll the logs and dust them with the powdered sugar.

Let the logs sit for 10 minutes to come to room temperature. Using a serrated knife, cut each log into ¼-inch slices, and enjoy.

Store in an airtight container in the fridge for up to 10 days (I like to pre-cut my salami logs so that I can enjoy a sweet treat any time of the day without needing to take out a knife every time).

NOTES:

If you don't have a food processor, crush the cookies with a mortar and pestle or transfer them to a large zip-seal bag and break them up using a rolling pin or a heavy-bottomed glass or cup.

You can use any unsweetened nondairy milk you like in this recipe, except for canned coconut milk (coconut beverage from a carton works great, though).

Here are variations you can make to the recipe:

- *Replace some of the cookies with toasted chopped nuts or slivered almonds, as long as you have a total weight of 7 oz (200 g).*

- *Substitute cranberries and raisins with chopped dried apricots or prunes.*

- *Fold ½ teaspoon of orange zest in along with the crushed cookies and dried fruits.*

- *For festive dessert kolbasa, add 1 to 2 teaspoons of Grand Marnier, bourbon, Amaretto, or brown rum to the chocolate mixture before folding in the cookies and dried fruits.*

- *If you do not eat gluten, opt for gluten-free cookies.*

Queen Elizabeth Cake

(NUT/SEED-FREE)

MAKES: ONE 9-INCH CAKE
PREPARATION: 15 MINUTES
COOKING: 30 MINUTES
RESTING: 15 MINUTES

QUEEN ELIZABETH CAKE is a cake that originated in Canada, and some speculate that it was created in honor of Queen Elizabeth II's coronation. My family has been making a version of this cake for over two decades, and we especially enjoy it during the colder months, with a cup of coffee or tea. To me, this cake rhymes with pure comfort and coziness. It is incredibly moist and tender. The flavor of the dates is subtle yet adds caramel hints to the sponge, while the coconut topping adds bite and texture, balancing out the softness of the sponge.

○ ○

CAKE

1 packed cup (7 oz/200 g) dates of choice, pitted and coarsely chopped (see note)

1 cup (150 ml) boiling water

1 tsp baking soda

1 tbsp (10 g) ground chia or flax seeds

3 tbsp (45 ml) water

1 cup (140 g) whole-wheat flour

½ cup (70 g) all-purpose flour (see note)

1 tsp baking powder

¼ tsp sea salt

⅓ cup (67 g) organic cane sugar

¼ cup (60 g) unsalted vegan butter, at room temperature

1 tsp vanilla extract

○ ○ ○

PREPARE THE CAKE

Preheat the oven to 375°F. Grease a 9-inch springform pan with cooking spray. Line the bottom of the pan with a round of parchment paper.

Place the dates, boiling water, and baking soda in a bowl. Stir, cover with a plate, and set aside for 5 minutes.

In a small bowl, whisk together the ground chia seeds and water. Set aside.

In a large bowl, whisk together the whole-wheat flour, all-purpose flour, baking powder, and salt. Set aside.

In a separate bowl and using an electric mixer, cream together the cane sugar and butter until light and fluffy. Add the chia mixture and vanilla extract, and whisk to incorporate.

To the flour mixture, add the butter mixture and the soaked dates (and their soaking water). Whisk until no streaks of flour remain. Pour into the prepared springform pan and smooth the top.

Bake for 20 to 25 minutes, until a toothpick inserted into the center comes out clean. Remove the cake from the oven, poke the top 2 dozen times with a toothpick, and set aside, still in its pan.

CONTINUED ➤

⅓ cup (67 g) brown sugar

6 tbsp (90 ml) full-fat coconut milk

2 tbsp (30 g) unsalted vegan butter

⅓ cup (35 g) unsweetened shredded coconut (see note)

PREPARE THE COCONUT TOPPING

In a small saucepan, bring the brown sugar, coconut milk, and butter to a boil over high heat, stirring often with a silicone spatula to help the sugar melt.

Reduce the heat to low and simmer for about 4 minutes or until the mixture has thickened enough to coat the back of a spoon.

Remove the caramel from the heat and fold in the shredded coconut.

Pour the coconut topping over the cake and spread it in an even layer.

Place the cake on a parchment-lined baking sheet.

Return the cake to the oven, turn the oven to broil (500°F), and broil for 2 to 3 minutes, until the topping is bubbling and the coconut is golden brown. Remove from the oven and place on a cooling rack.

Let cool for 15 minutes, then gently release the springform pan. Let the cake cool further on the cooling rack. The cake can be enjoyed warm or completely cooled. Store in the fridge in an airtight container for up to 3 days.

NOTES:

This recipe works well with Medjool or Noor dates.

If you'd prefer to make the cake using only whole-wheat flour, simply substitute it for the all-purpose flour, using 1½ cups (210 g) of whole-wheat flour in total, and bake the cake for 25 to 30 minutes.

I grew up eating this cake with walnuts in the coconut topping, so if you'd like to and are not nut intolerant, fold in ¼ cup (30 g) of chopped walnuts along with the coconut before spreading the topping on the cake.

Decadent Hazelnut Bites

(GLUTEN-FREE)   (EXTRA PREP)

MAKES: 20 BITES
PREPARATION: 30 MINUTES
COOKING: 20 MINUTES
RESTING: 4 HOURS

○ ○

1 cup (175 g) vegan chocolate
  chips, plus 1 cup (175 g) for
  coating, optional (see note)

¼ cup (60 ml) hazelnut butter
  (I love Prana's Organic
  Hazelnut Butter)

6 tbsp (90 ml) full-fat coconut
  milk

Pinch of sea salt

½ cup (75 g) raw hazelnuts
  (see note)

½ cup (15 g) Rice Chex cereal
  (see note)

Chopped hazelnuts, for sprinkling,
  optional

○

WHEN I WAS growing up, Ferrero Rocher was a classic treat during the holiday season. My mom would always offer my brothers and me a box of these chocolatey hazelnut delights. Unfortunately, after turning vegan, I could no longer take part in this tradition. I decided that, while I wait for Ferrero to release a vegan alternative, I would make my own. These bites require a little extra love and attention to put together than does purchasing a ready-made box. Take your time melting the rich filling, individually stuffing each treat with a toasted hazelnut, covering them in a wafer layer and chopped hazelnut bits, and, finally, coating them with glossy melted chocolate. These chocolates are perfect as a gift, but to be quite honest, they might just be best kept for yourself!

○ ○ ○

Preheat the oven to 350°F.

Place 1 cup (175 g) of chocolate chips, the hazelnut butter, and coconut milk in a large, heatproof mixing bowl. To make a double boiler, fill a medium saucepan (big enough to hold your bowl without having it touch the bottom) with 1 inch of water. Set the bowl with the chocolate mixture on top of the saucepan and heat on medium-low heat to melt the chocolate evenly. Stir in the salt.

Let the mixture cool for 10 minutes, then cover and place in the fridge until set, at least 3 hours.

Roast the hazelnuts in a baking dish until the skin peels off easily and they are becoming golden and fragrant, about 10 minutes. Let cool completely before removing as much of the skin as possible by rubbing them with your fingers.

Set aside 20 hazelnuts. Chop the remainder into small pieces and transfer to a bowl. Set aside.

Crush the Rice Chex using a mortar and pestle or by adding them to the bowl with the hazelnuts and pressing on them using the bottom of a mug. You are not looking to crush them into a powdery form, but rather into pumpkin seed–sized pieces. Toss together with the chopped hazelnuts.

CONTINUED ➤

Once the chocolate filling has set (with a texture thicker than margarine), remove it from the fridge. Line a plate with parchment paper.

Scoop about a tablespoon-worth of the filling into your hand. Place a roasted hazelnut in the middle of it and roll the mixture between your hands to form a ball. Set on the prepared plate. Repeat the process with the remaining whole hazelnuts, using up all the filling.

Gently drop the balls, one or two at a time, into the Chex mixture and gently press the coating onto each ball, encasing them in a crust. Place on the plate and refrigerate for 30 minutes.

OPTIONAL EXTRA COATING

Melt the remaining 1 cup (175 g) of chocolate chips in the bowl of a double boiler set over medium heat until silky smooth.

Gently drop a chilled hazelnut ball into the mixture, toss to coat, and scoop out using a fork. Give the ball a little shake to remove any excess chocolate and place back on the plate. Sprinkle with chopped hazelnuts, if desired.

Repeat the process with the remaining balls.

Refrigerate the balls again until the chocolate is set, about 15 minutes, then enjoy.

Store in the fridge in an airtight container for up to 1 week.

NOTES:

For the vegan chocolate chips, I like to use a 50-50 mix of semisweet and 70% dark because this combo reminds me the most of the traditional Ferrero Rocher pralines. However, if you want a sweeter treat, use only semisweet vegan chocolate chips. If you want something a bit more bitter, use only 70% dark vegan chocolate chips.

If you are using toasted hazelnuts, skip the roasting step.

If you do not have Rice Chex cereal at home, roast an additional ½ cup (75 g) of hazelnuts and crush them using a mortar and pestle into small pieces. Coat each treat with it as your crispy layer, gently pressing the roasted hazelnuts into the chocolate filling to help them stick.

Grand Marnier Crepe Cake

(NUT/SEED-FREE) (EXTRA PREP)

MAKES: ONE 9-INCH CAKE
PREPARATION: 30 MINUTES
COOKING: 1 HOUR
RESTING: 3 HOURS

CREPE CAKES ARE one of my favorite showstopper cakes. All your careful time and attention needed to make the cake pays off the moment you slice into it and see all the beautiful layers of crepe hugged by rich cream. This recipe is inspired by my love of the chocolate-orange flavor combination. I first had my mind blown by it in my late teenage years when I made a batch of Grand Marnier brownies, which were the perfect marriage of rich dark chocolate and bright, citrusy, sweet, and slightly bitter liqueur. Here, the base of My Mom's Classic Crepes (p. 35) is elevated by the rich, smooth, and sweet chocolate-orange frosting. This cake is a celebration cake, perfect for birthdays and special holidays.

○ ○

My Mom's Classic Crepes (p. 35), about 18 crepes if using ¼ cup of batter per crepe (see note on page 36)

The Best Chocolate Frosting (p. 272), doubled, Grand Marnier version (see notes on page 272), chilled for at least 3 hours

Orange segments, membranes removed, for garnish

Chocolate shavings, for garnish

○ ○ ○

To assemble, place a crepe on a serving plate and spread 1 heaping tablespoon of frosting on it, reaching the edges.

Top with another crepe and frosting. Repeat the process with the remaining crepes and frosting.

Garnish with orange segments and chocolate shavings.

Enjoy after assembling or store in the fridge in an airtight container, or loosely covered with foil, for up to 3 days.

Fried Banana Beignets

(NUT/SEED-FREE) (EXTRA PREP)

MAKES: 4–6 SERVINGS
PREPARATION: 15 MINUTES
COOKING: 30 MINUTES
RESTING: 1 HOUR 30 MINUTES

I HAVE A CLEAR and vivid memory of a day when I was about seven years old, living in Pointe-Noire, Congo, through yet another power outage. To distract me, my mom bought me my favorite fried banana donuts from a local vendor. When I took a bite into that donut, I connected to the true power of food and realized how it can add light to dark situations and create a beautiful, long-lasting memory out of it. This donut recipe is my little offer of light, reminding you that simple ingredients like bananas, flour, and sugar can be transformed with a little love into a decadent treat to bring joy to your day. These donuts are probably not made exactly like they were back in Pointe-Noire, but I did consult with a few banana beignet experts to make sure these are up to par.

2 very ripe bananas (8 oz/230 g), peeled

1 cup lukewarm water (at about 120°F)

¼ cup (50 g) organic cane granulated sugar

¼ tsp sea salt

1¼ tsp instant dry active yeast

¼ tsp ground cinnamon, optional

2¾ cups (385 g) all-purpose flour, divided

5–6 cups (1.25–1.5 L) canola oil, for frying

Blend the bananas in a mini food processor or high-speed blender until smooth. Alternatively, you can mash them well using a fork.

In a large bowl, whisk together the water, sugar, and salt until the sugar has dissolved.

Sprinkle the yeast overtop of the water mixture. Let sit for 5 minutes or until the yeast has activated and is foamy.

Pour in the banana puree and incorporate the cinnamon, if using, and 2 cups of flour, ½ cup (70 g) at a time, stirring with a whisk in between each addition, until the mixture is smooth. Then pour in the remaining ¾ cup (105 g) of flour, ¼ cup (35 g) at a time, continuing to incorporate the flour, this time using a wooden spoon or silicone spatula to mix well between each addition.

Cover the bowl tightly with plastic film and a clean kitchen towel. Let the dough rise in a warm environment (see note) for 1 hour 30 minutes or until it has doubled in size and is bubbly.

Fill a deep pot with 5 to 6 cups of canola oil, making sure to leave 2 inches of space from the top. Heat over medium heat until it reaches 350°F. If you do not have a thermometer, carefully drop a bit of dough into the oil: if the oil sizzles and the dough floats to the top, it is hot enough for your beignets.

CONTINUED ➤

Line a plate or baking sheet with paper towel and fill a bowl with water. Place this next to your frying station.

Wet your dominant hand in the bowl of water and scoop out some of the dough (see note). Gently drop it into the hot oil, being careful not to splatter the hot oil.

Repeat to fill the pot, but do not overcrowd it. I suggest wetting your hands each time before you scoop the beignet dough, to prevent the dough from sticking to your fingers too much. Fry the beignets until golden brown, then flip and fry on the second side.

Using a slotted spoon, transfer the beignets to the prepared plate or baking sheet. Repeat the process with the remaining batter.

Enjoy these beignets warm or at room temperature. Store at room temperature in an airtight container for up to 3 days.

NOTES:

My dad's friend traditionally makes these donuts by mixing the dough in a large pot, then covering the pot with its lid and putting it outside for the dough rise in the heat of the Congo summer sun. If you're making these on a cold day, heat the oven to 150°F, then turn off the oven and turn on the oven light. Place the dough in the oven, covered with a plastic wrap and a clean kitchen towel.

If you do not want to use your hands to make these, you can use two tablespoons instead—one to scoop out the dough and the other to push the dough into the oil.

If you're looking for sweeter beignets, immediately after frying, toss them in a mixture of organic cane sugar and ground cinnamon.

Nut-Free Tiramisu

(NUT/SEED-FREE) (EXTRA PREP)

MAKES: 8 SERVINGS
PREPARATION: 30 MINUTES
COOKING: 45 MINUTES
RESTING: 24 HOURS

WHILE TIRAMISU HAS a rich history in my relationship with Sam (it was the first edible gift I ever gave him), it took me writing this book to attempt creating a vegan version. It was a labor of love—the biggest challenge was ensuring that the sponge cake would shine the light on the true star of this dessert: the cream. To replicate mascarpone, I tapped into my creativity and blended together silken tofu and coconut cream. The result? A velvety smooth, subtly flavored cream that holds together beautifully when cut in to. As you prepare this dessert, I encourage you to savor every step, from preparing the sponge to baking it and dipping it into the warm coffee, covering it with luscious cream, and finally garnishing your creation with a light dusting of cocoa. Trust that a few hours later, you will be able not only to enjoy a delightful vegan tiramisu but to taste all the love and attention you poured into this dessert.

SPONGE CAKE

1½ cups (210 g) all-purpose flour

¾ cup (150 g) organic cane sugar

¾ tsp baking soda

¾ tsp baking powder

¼ tsp sea salt

1 cup (250 ml) unsweetened soy milk

2 tbsp (30 ml) avocado oil

1½ tsp apple cider vinegar

1 tsp vanilla extract

2 cups (500 ml) strong coffee, warm

PREPARE THE SPONGE CAKE

Preheat the oven to 350°F. Brush an 8-inch square glass baking dish with a neutral cooking oil (such as avocado, canola, or melted refined coconut).

In a large mixing bowl, sift together the flour, cane sugar, baking soda, baking powder, and salt. Stir with a whisk.

Add the soy milk, avocado oil, apple cider vinegar, and vanilla extract. Whisk until smooth and no flour streaks remain, but be careful not to overmix.

Pour the batter into the prepared baking dish, smooth the top, and bake for 30 to 35 minutes, until the top is dry and a toothpick inserted into the center comes out clean.

Remove from the oven and let cool in the pan for 5 minutes, then transfer to a cooling rack and let cool until cool enough to handle, about 10 minutes.

CONTINUED ➤

CREAM

1 (10 oz/300 g) package silken tofu, drained

½ cup (56 g) powdered sugar

1 tsp vanilla extract

1 cup (250 ml) coconut cream, from a can

1 tbsp (5 g) Dutch-processed cocoa powder, for garnish

Cut the cake in half through the center using a serrated knife, creating 2 even layers. Cut each layer into 8 rectangles of equal size, giving you a total of 16 pieces.

Place the cake pieces on a parchment-lined baking sheet and bake for 10 minutes at 350°F.

Remove from the oven and let cool completely.

PREPARE THE CREAM

Blend the silken tofu, powdered sugar, and vanilla extract in a mini food processor or a high-speed blender until smooth. Set aside.

Scoop the thick coconut cream out of the can and into a mixing bowl. Using an electric mixer, whip it until fluffy. (Any leftover coconut water can be reserved for smoothies.)

Fold in the tofu mixture using a silicone spatula—at this point, the mixture will be fairly liquid.

ASSEMBLE THE CAKE

Pour the warm coffee into a deep bowl. Submerge a cake piece into the coffee for 10 seconds, so that the sponge absorbs the coffee.

Place the cake piece in the baking dish. Repeat the process with 7 more cake pieces, arranging them in a single layer in the baking dish.

Top this bottom layer of the tiramisu with half of the coconut cream mixture, spreading it in an even layer.

Dip the remaining 8 pieces of cake, one at a time, into the coffee, arranging them in a single layer on top of the cream layer. Top with the remaining coconut cream mixture.

Using a sifter, dust the tiramisu with the cocoa powder. Cover tightly with foil and chill in the fridge for at least 24 hours before enjoying. Store in the fridge, tightly covered with foil, for up to 4 days.

Spiced Poached Pear Puff Pastry Tart

(NUT/SEED-FREE) (EXTRA PREP)

MAKES: ONE 11- × 13-INCH TART
PREPARATION: 15 MINUTES
COOKING: 1 HOUR
RESTING: 30 MINUTES

2 cups (500 ml) water

½ cup (125 ml) maple syrup

1 large thumb (1 oz/30 g) of ginger, peeled and thinly sliced

½ tsp black pepper (see note)

6 firm Bosc pears (2 lbs/900 g), peeled, cored, and sliced ¼ inch thick

All-purpose flour, for dusting, optional

2 oz (350 g) vegan puff pastry, thawed (see note)

ONE OF MY MOM'S go-to desserts whenever she hosts us is a simple sliced-pear puff pastry tart. This easy-to-make fruit-forward dessert is always a crowd-pleaser. This recipe is a variation of my mom's. I've added one extra step to the tart-making process: poaching the pears in a maple syrup, ginger, and black pepper liquid. I love watching over my pears as they are poached, carefully moving them around in the sweet and spicy mixture. I encourage you to give the pear slices a try once they are poached and notice how the flavor has changed. The maple syrup infuses extra sweetness to the pears, while the ginger and black pepper add a nice kick. Once the tart has baked in the oven, it is finished with a drizzle of the poaching liquid, now reduced to a luscious sweet and spiced caramel.

In a large saucepan, place the water, maple syrup, sliced ginger, and pepper. Give it all a stir using a silicone spatula, then gently drop in the pears. Stir and bring to a boil over high heat, uncovered.

Reduce the heat to low and simmer, uncovered, for 10 minutes, stirring occasionally.

Using a slotted spoon, transfer the pear slices to a bowl. Place in the fridge to cool for 30 minutes.

In the meantime, increase the heat to medium-high and cook the poaching liquid until it has reduced by more than half and thickened to a maple syrup–like consistency, about 15 to 20 minutes, stirring occasionally. Transfer to a small bowl. Set aside.

Preheat the oven to 400°F. Line a baking sheet with parchment paper or a silicone mat.

If you're using puff pastry that needs to be rolled out, lightly dust flour on a clean work surface and roll the puff pastry out into an 11- × 13-inch rectangle, then transfer to the prepared baking sheet. Alternatively, if your puff pastry is already rolled out, measure an 11- × 13-inch rectangle and simply place it on your prepared baking sheet.

CONTINUED ➤

Place the cooled poached pears on the puff pastry, leaving a ½-inch border all around.

Bake for 30 to 35 minutes, until the edges and bottom of the tart are golden brown.

Remove from the oven and let cool completely, then drizzle the reduced spicy poaching liquid onto the tart (see note). Cut into pieces and enjoy.

You can store in the fridge in an airtight container for up to 3 days, just note that the texture of the tart will soften with time.

NOTES:

I strongly suggest using freshly ground pepper in this recipe as opposed to pepper powder. This will result in a much more robust and aromatic pepper flavor.

Fun fact: Many commercial puff pastry brands are actually vegan! They do not use dairy butter in their dough. So vegans can still enjoy puff pastry, minus the dairy products! My go-to brands are Tenderflake and 7Days Bake It. If you're looking for vegan puff pastry, make sure its ingredient list does not include dairy butter.

If your reduced poaching liquid has thickened too much while cooling, reheat it in the microwave on medium power for 15 seconds, or until liquefied, before drizzling it onto your tart. This mixture can also be used to sweeten your chai tea.

Date-Sweetened Chocolate Cream Tarts

(CUSTOMIZABLE) (GLUTEN-FREE)
(NUT/SEED-FREE) (EXTRA PREP)

MAKES: FOUR 5-INCH MINI
TARTS OR ONE 9-INCH TART
PREPARATION: 15 MINUTES
COOKING: 10 MINUTES
RESTING: 1–2 HOURS

○

IF THERE IS one thing that makes me happy, it's having a crowd devour one of my dishes, especially one that truly feels unique to me. That was the case when I shared a variation of these tarts, covered with fresh juicy blueberries, with Sam's family. It was a hot summer night and I was in charge of dessert, so I prepared these tarts, as I knew everyone would appreciate a cold yet rich and chocolatey treat that featured in-season blueberries. It was gone in minutes! The entire experience reminded me of making crepes for my family at age twelve; it brought me so much joy to have my loved ones gather together and savor a dish I had poured love into making. Whether you make these tarts for yourself or for people you love, I encourage you to slow down and take your time with the ingredients and treasure the steps required to bring this recipe to life.

○ ○

CRUST

1½ cups (170 g) tigernut flour
(see note)

2 tbsp + 1 tsp (15 g) Dutch-
processed cocoa powder

¼ tsp sea salt

5 tbsp (70 g) hardened refined
coconut oil

1 tbsp (15 ml) maple syrup

○ ○ ○

PREPARE THE CRUST

Preheat the oven to 350°F.

In a large bowl, mix together the tigernut flour, cocoa powder, and salt until combined, making sure to break down any bigger clumps of flour.

Add the coconut oil and maple syrup and incorporate using a fork or a pastry cutter.

Use your hands to form a ball with the dough, then flatten it into a thick disc. If you are making mini tarts, divide the dough into four. Transfer the dough to the mini tart pans with removable bottoms (or to a single tart pan), pressing the mixture evenly into the bottoms and up the sides.

Poke the crusts with a fork and bake for 8 minutes. Remove from the oven and let cool completely.

CONTINUED ➤

FILLING

½ cup (3½ oz/100 g) packed pitted dates (such as Bam, Medjool, or Habibi)

5 oz (150 g) silken tofu, drained

½ cup (60 g) chopped dark chocolate (at least 70%; I used 85%), plus more for garnish

¼ cup (60 ml) full-fat coconut milk

1 tbsp (5 g) Dutch-processed cocoa powder

½ tsp instant coffee powder, optional

Pinch of sea salt

Fresh berries (sliced strawberries, blueberries, halved blackberries or raspberries), for garnish

PREPARE THE FILLING

Place the dates in a bowl and cover them with boiling water. Let sit for 10 minutes. Drain and gently squeeze out any excess water (you can reserve the date water to use in smoothie or oatmeal recipes).

Transfer the dates to a high-speed blender and add the tofu, chocolate, coconut milk, cocoa powder, coffee powder, and salt. Blend until smooth, scraping down the sides of the blender as needed to make sure all the bits and pieces are well blended.

ASSEMBLE THE TARTS

Pour the filling into the tart crusts. Smooth out the tops using a silicone spatula or the back of a spoon.

If you're making 4 mini tarts, chill in the fridge for at least 1 hour, uncovered. If you're making 1 big tart, chill for at least 2 hours.

To serve, carefully remove the tarts from their pans and garnish with fresh berries and chopped dark chocolate. Store in the fridge in an airtight container for up to 3 days.

NOTES:

Feel free to replace the tigernut flour with an equal amount of almond flour.

Pomegranate arils are another garnish option for these tarts.

The Chocolate Microwave Cake of Your Dreams

(CUSTOMIZABLE)

MAKES: 1 MUG CAKE
PREPARATION: 5 MINUTES
COOKING: 2 MINUTES

○○

2 tbsp (17 g) whole-wheat flour

1 tbsp + 2 tsp (10 g) Dutch-processed cocoa powder

1 tbsp (7 g) tigernut flour (see note)

¼ tsp baking powder

Pinch of sea salt

3 tbsp (45 ml) unsweetened soy milk

1 tbsp (15 ml) hazelnut butter (see note)

1 tbsp (15 ml) maple syrup

1 tsp vanilla extract

2 tbsp (30 ml) dairy-free 50–70% chocolate chips

○

I KNOW WHAT you might be thinking: "I have tried many microwave cakes, and none of them were as satisfying as they claimed to be." Rest assured, my friend, this one is about to change things for the better. Ready in under 10 minutes and requiring only ten ingredients, this recipe is one of my go-tos when I want a rich, luxurious weeknight treat but also want to slow down and prepare a single-serving dessert as an act of self-care. This cake is chocolatey and decadent, and melts in your mouth. Making—and eating—it is one of my favorite ways to unwind after a long workday. I almost always pair it with a glass of cold soy milk!

○○○

In a mug, mix together the whole-wheat flour, cocoa powder, tigernut flour, baking powder, and salt, using a small whisk or a fork.

Add the soy milk, hazelnut butter, maple syrup, and vanilla extract. Mix well to fully combine.

Fold in the chocolate chips.

Microwave on high power for 1 minute 15 seconds (see note). Let cool slightly, then enjoy warm with a glass of nondairy milk.

NOTES:

If you don't have tigernut flour, use instead an equal amount of either whole-wheat flour, almond flour, or brown rice flour. I find that the tigernut flour adds texture to this cake, which is why I use it, but it is not necessary.

My favorite nut butter for this recipe is hazelnut butter because it complements chocolate so well, but feel free to use any other natural, smooth, and unflavored nut butter you have on hand.

This cooking time is based on my microwave's power of 1,000 watts. If your microwave's power is less, or if you notice that your cake looks underdone (the top is not set), microwave it for another 15 seconds. If your microwave's power is higher than 1,000 watts, start by microwaving your cake for 45 seconds and add more time as needed, in 15 seconds increments, checking your cake between each increment.

Peanut Butter Pouding Chômeur

(EXTRA PREP)

MAKES: 8 SERVINGS
PREPARATION: 10 MINUTES
COOKING: 40 MINUTES
RESTING: 1 HOUR

○ ○

1 tbsp (10 g) ground chia or flax
  seeds

3 tbsp (45 ml) water

1 cup (250 ml) maple syrup

1 cup (250 ml) full-fat coconut
  milk, from a can

¼ cup (70 g) smooth natural
  peanut butter (see note)

¼ cup (57 g) softened unsalted
  vegan butter

¼ cup (40 g) brown sugar

1 tsp vanilla extract

1 cup (120 g) spelt flour or
  whole-wheat flour

1½ tsp baking powder

Pinch of sea salt

½ cup (125 ml) unsweetened
  soy milk

Chopped peanuts, for garnish,
  optional

○

POUDING CHÔMEUR IS a dessert I first became familiar with when I moved to Montreal. Directly translated to English, the French name means "unemployed pudding." It was created in Quebec during the Great Depression and has been a classic ever since. Simply put, it's a cake atop sweet maple sauce. If you are looking for a recipe to satisfy an intense sweet craving, this is *it*. My version's sauce, unlike the original, contains peanut butter, making it thicker and richer, and preventing the cake from being totally soaked. My favorite step in preparing this cake? Spooning the batter onto the caramel. It is incredibly satisfying to watch it float there, surrounded by all that rich maple goodness.

○ ○ ○

Preheat the oven to 400°F.

In a small bowl, whisk together the ground chia seeds and water. Set aside.

In a small saucepan, bring the maple syrup, coconut milk, and peanut butter to a boil over high heat, whisking often to incorporate the peanut butter until mostly homogeneous—it's okay if some chunks of peanut butter have not fully been incorporated. Pour the mixture into a 5- × 9-inch loaf pan.

In a large bowl, use an electric mixer to beat the butter and brown sugar on high speed for 1 to 2 minutes, until the mixture is fluffy. Whisk in the chia mixture and vanilla extract.

In a separate large bowl, mix together the spelt flour, baking powder, and salt. Add to the butter mixture. Pour in the soy milk and mix to incorporate all the ingredients. Using a tablespoon, spoon the batter onto the maple mixture, leaving the dollops untouched.

Place the pan on a baking sheet and bake for 25 to 30 minutes. Let cool on a cooling rack for 1 to 3 hours, to allow the maple mixture to thicken.

Serve at room temperature or warm, garnished with chopped peanuts, if desired. Store in the fridge, tightly covered with foil, for up to 3 days. Reheat each piece slightly in the microwave, at medium power for 15 seconds, before serving again.

NOTE:

You can use the nut butter of your choice instead of peanut butter. The best alternatives for this recipe are almond butter and cashew butter; just make sure they are smooth and contain no added ingredients (like oil, sugar, or salt).

Maple Apple Galette

(NUT/SEED-FREE) (EXTRA PREP)

MAKES: ONE 11-INCH GALETTE
PREPARATION: 30 MINUTES
COOKING: 55 MINUTES
RESTING: 1 HOUR

○

I AM NO PIE EXPERT—at all. There is something about pies that I find quite intimidating! That's why, when I crave a pie and don't have the courage to try making one myself, I opt to bake a galette instead. Just like a traditional pie, a galette requires you to consciously slow down as you prepare its various elements (the crust and filling) and assemble them. My favorite part of making galettes is folding over the edges of the crust, as if tucking in my fruits with a buttery blanket. Inspired by Canadian flavors and ingredients, this galette features my own homemade Maple Butter (p. 265), as well as local apples. The crust is light and buttery, and the aroma of maple is present through every element. The filling is simple yet satisfying—*and*, of course, inspired by apple pies. It is a great dessert to enjoy in the fall when there is an abundance of apples!

○ ○

CRUST

1½ cups (210 g) all-purpose flour, plus more as needed

¼ tsp sea salt

6 tbsp (90 g) cold unsalted vegan butter, cubed

2 tbsp (30 ml) Maple Butter (p. 265) (see note)

4–5 tbsp (60–75 ml) ice cold water (see note)

○ ○ ○

PREPARE THE CRUST

In a large bowl, whisk together the all-purpose flour and salt to evenly distribute the salt. Add the butter and maple butter and incorporate using a pastry cutter or a fork until the mixture has a soft, sandy texture. Alternatively, in a food processor, pulse together the flour and salt until well combined, then pulse in the butter and maple butter. Transfer the mixture to a large bowl.

Add 4 tablespoons of ice cold water, 1 tablespoon (15 ml) at a time, mixing with a silicone spatula to incorporate after each addition, until the dough sticks together enough to form a ball. If the dough is still pretty crumbly, add the remaining 1 tablespoon of water. If your mixture becomes too sticky, add 1 teaspoon (3 g) of all-purpose flour and incorporate it into the dough.

Form the dough into a ball with your hands, then wrap in plastic wrap. Place in the fridge to chill for up to 1 hour, while you prepare the galette filling.

CONTINUED ➤

FILLING

1 tbsp (15 g) unsalted vegan butter

5 baking apples (33½ oz/950 g), peeled, cored, and sliced ¼ inch thick (see note)

3 tbsp (45 ml) Maple Butter (p. 265), plus more for drizzling (see note)

Pinch of sea salt

1 tbsp (15 ml) unsweetened soy milk, for garnish

1 tbsp (15 ml) maple syrup, for garnish

Maple sugar, for garnish, optional (see note)

PREPARE THE FILLING

Melt the unsalted butter in a large saucepan set over medium heat.

Add the apples, maple butter, and salt. Cook, stirring often, for 5 to 8 minutes, until the apples are softened but still have a bite to them—you do not want them to be mushy.

Increase the heat to high and continue to cook for 1 to 2 minutes, until the liquid has been mostly absorbed by the apples. Remove from the heat and let cool for 10 minutes.

Preheat the oven to 375°F.

In a small bowl, mix together the soy milk and maple syrup. Set aside.

ASSEMBLE THE GALETTE

Lightly sprinkle flour onto a piece of parchment paper large enough to fit your baking sheet.

Place the chilled galette dough in the middle of the parchment and roll it out into a circle 12 inches in diameter. Transfer the parchment paper and dough onto the baking sheet.

Scoop the apple filling into the middle of the dough circle, leaving behind the excess juices if there are any. Leave a 1-inch border all around.

Fold over the edges of the crust, and brush the exposed edges with the maple syrup mixture.

Sprinkle the crust with maple sugar, if using. Bake the galette for 45 minutes, until the edges are golden. For extra color, once the galette is fully baked, increase the temperature to 500°F and broil for 1 to 2 minutes, watching closely so it doesn't burn.

Let the galette cool for at least 30 minutes before drizzling with additional maple butter and eating. If your maple butter is too thick to drizzle, warm it in the microwave for a few seconds first.

Store in the fridge in an airtight container for up to 3 days.

NOTES:

Feel free to replace the homemade maple butter in this recipe with store-bought.

For really cold water, add ice cubes to a glass of water and let chill.

In terms of apple choice, I love to use a variety in this galette to create more flavor. My go-tos for baking are Granny Smith, Honeycrisp, and Pink Lady.

If you don't have maple sugar, swap it out with turbinado sugar or, if you eat nuts, sprinkle sliced almonds around the galette's edges.

The Only Chocolate Chip Cookies I Will Ever Make

(CUSTOMIZABLE)   (GLUTEN-FREE)
(EXTRA PREP)

MAKES: 16 COOKIES
PREPARATION: 10 MINUTES
COOKING: 15 MINUTES
RESTING: 2 HOURS

THIS RECIPE IS dedicated to Sam, who would be happy eating one dessert for the rest of his life: chocolate chip cookies. When I first tried making these cookies, I never imagined something like this could come out of my kitchen. They are crispy on the outside and chewy in the middle, and have a lovely balance of saltiness, sweetness, and slight earthiness. The dough for these cookies is quite different from others in that it is rather dry. This means that, as you prepare them, you will have to use your hands a little to mix in the flour and form the cookies. Embrace the process, and think of it as connecting to your food and using your hands to shape these cookies into life.

2 cups (180 g) chickpea flour

⅓ cup (67 g) organic cane sugar

¼ cup (40 g) brown sugar

1 tsp baking powder

½ tsp baking soda

⅓ cup (75 g) melted unsalted vegan butter (see note)

⅓ cup (80 ml) tahini (see note)

¼ cup (60 ml) unsweetened soy milk

1 tbsp (15 ml) dark miso paste (see note)

⅔–¾ cup (100 g) chocolate pieces (see note)

Fleur de sel or Maldon salt, for sprinkling

In a large mixing bowl, whisk together the chickpea flour, cane sugar, brown sugar, baking powder, and baking soda to combine.

In a blender, blend the butter, tahini, soy milk, and miso on medium speed until smooth. Alternatively, you can whisk the ingredients together by hand until smooth.

Pour the wet mixture into the dry mixture, and combine using a silicone spatula, pressing the mixture against the sides of the bowl until no streaks of flour remain. At this point, the mixture will not be soft and smooth but rather very crumbly—that is completely normal. I find that using my hands to help the mixture come together works really well.

Fold in the chocolate. Cover the bowl with plastic wrap and refrigerate for at least 2 hours and up to 24 hours (see note).

Preheat the oven to 350°F. Line a baking sheet with parchment paper or a silicone mat.

CONTINUED ➤

Scoop the dough into 2-tablespoon portions and place them on the baking sheet, spacing the cookies about 1 inch apart. If the texture is still a little crumbly, just squeeze the cookie dough together, using your hands to form balls.

Bake for 15 minutes or until the cookies have spread, browned around the edges, and feel dry and slightly crispy to the touch.

Remove the cookies from the oven and let cool on the baking sheet for at least 15 minutes.

Sprinkle with fleur de sel and enjoy. Store at room temperature in an airtight container for up to 3 days.

NOTES:

If you don't have butter, this recipe works great with avocado oil or canola oil as well.

When choosing your tahini, opt for one that is light in color and smooth in texture. I like to buy the imports from the Middle East, which are quite easy to find at most large grocery chains. Or, if you don't have tahini, opt for a smooth and natural (this is a must!) nut or seed butter of your choice.

You can use either dark or light miso paste. Just know that the darker the miso, the more pronounced the flavor.

I like to use an equal mix of vegan chocolate chips and chopped dark (85%) chocolate, but feel free to use any combination you prefer.

Refrigerating the dough does two things: it helps it hold together, making the scooping easier, and it gives it time for the flavors of the miso and tahini to develop. I suggest waiting a minimum of 2 hours before baking the cookies, and waiting 15 minutes before trying one, as they will be rather soft right out of the oven.

Olive Oil and Rose Polenta Bundt Cake

NUT/SEED-FREE

MAKES: 8–10 SERVINGS
PREPARATION: 10 MINUTES
COOKING: 40 MINUTES

LIGHT, SOFT, AND DELICATE in flavor, this Bundt cake is the perfect dessert to make when you are looking for a quick one that is not rich or creamy, and which will pair beautifully with a cup of tea or coffee. The fine cornmeal (or polenta) in this cake gives it a nice bite and a lovely, slightly crumbly, texture, while the all-purpose flour keeps it soft and fluffy. My favorite way to slow down when making this cake: smelling the aroma of the rosewater as it is incorporated into the cake batter. The combination of the earthy, grassy flavor of the olive oil, along with the delicate floral taste of the rosewater, gives this cake a really refined flavor profile, making it hard to stop eating at only one slice!

1 cup (140 g) fine polenta (#400 fine cornmeal)

1 cup (140 g) all-purpose flour

2 tsp baking powder

¼ tsp sea salt

¾ cup (185 ml) unsweetened soy milk

⅔ cup (150 g) organic cane sugar

½ cup (125 ml) extra virgin olive oil (see note)

2½ tsp rosewater (see note)

Powdered sugar, for dusting, optional

Preheat the oven to 350°F. Brush generously a 6-cup Bundt pan with olive oil.

In a large mixing bowl, whisk together the polenta, flour, baking powder, and salt.

In a separate large mixing bowl, whisk together the soy milk, sugar, olive oil, and rosewater until most of the sugar has dissolved.

Add the dry mixture to the liquid mixture, and whisk until incorporated and no large lumps remain.

Pour the batter into the Bundt pan, smooth the top, and bake for 35 to 40 minutes, until the edges are golden brown and a toothpick inserted into the center comes out clean.

Let cool in the pan on a cooling rack for 10 minutes. Remove from the cake pan and let cool on the rack for another 20 minutes before slicing. If dusting with powdered sugar, wait until the cake is completely cool before sifting some onto your cake.

Store the cake at room temperature in an airtight container for up to 2 days.

NOTES:

If you prefer a milder olive oil flavor, choose an olive oil that is labeled light taste *or* extra mild taste.

If you don't have rosewater, you can swap it out with 2 teaspoons of orange blossom water.

Napoleon Cake

(NUT/SEED-FREE) (EXTRA PREP)

MAKES: 8–10 SERVINGS
PREPARATION: 30 MINUTES
COOKING: 1 HOUR
RESTING: 12 HOURS

○

NAPOLEON CAKE IS a common dessert in Russian and Ukrainian households, and practically every family has their own version. In my family, this cake is a *legend*. Ours has undergone quite a big transformation over the years, first made with lots of dairy, now fully plant-based. Nonetheless, it remains complex in flavor, soft, pillowy, and creamy! Made of carefully rolled-out layers of vegan puff pastry and a scrumptious sweet vanilla cream, the Napoleon is the cake I turn to when I want to impress a crowd, or sometimes to just treat myself and Sam to a luxurious dessert.

○ ○

CREAM

¼ cup (30 g) cornstarch (see note)

1¼ cups (310 ml) unsweetened soy milk

1 cup (250 ml) full-fat coconut milk, from a can

½ cup (125 ml) maple syrup

1½ tbsp (22 ml) vanilla extract

PUFF PASTRY LAYERS

1 (14 oz/397 g) package vegan puff pastry, thawed (see note)

All-purpose flour, for dusting

○ ○ ○

PREPARE THE CREAM

In a saucepan, whisk together the cornstarch, soy milk, coconut milk, and maple syrup until smooth. Bring to a gentle simmer over medium-high heat, stirring constantly with a whisk. Reduce the heat to medium-low and, still stirring, cook until thickened—it should coat the back of a spoon.

Remove from the heat and transfer to a bowl. Stir in the vanilla extract. Cover the bowl with plastic wrap, gently pressing on the wrap so that it touches the cream. Refrigerate until cool, about 2 hours.

PREPARE THE PUFF PASTRY LAYERS

Preheat the oven to 400°F. Line two baking sheets with parchment paper or silicone mats.

Divide the puff pastry into 4 equal pieces.

Flour a clean work surface and roll out one of the pieces until the dough is 1 mm thick.

Use a 9-inch cake pan to cut out a circle in the dough. Place the dough circle on one of the prepared baking sheets. Poke it half a dozen times with a fork.

Repeat the process with the remaining puff pastry pieces. Be sure to flour your work surface and rolling pin as needed to prevent the dough from sticking.

CONTINUED ➤

Bake the puff pastry on the middle rack for 12 to 14 minutes, until golden brown and cooked through. You will need to do this in two batches, since you are working with two baking sheets.

Let the baked puff pastry layers cool completely on a cooling rack.

Once your first baking sheet is out of the oven, gather the excess puff pastry into a ball and roll out into a thin 10-inch circle. Using the cake pan, cut out a circle in the dough. Transfer this extra layer to the baking sheet.

Place the excess pieces of puff pastry on the baking sheet; you will use them to decorate your cake.

Bake for 12 to 14 minutes. Transfer to a cooling rack to cool completely.

ASSEMBLE THE CAKE

Using a whisk, mix the chilled cream until smooth—there might still be a few lumps left after stirring, but don't worry, you won't be able to tell they are there once the cake has set.

Using a serrated knife, cut any puff pastry layers that have puffed up by more than a ¼ inch (the ones that have formed a dome) in half horizontally—generally I need to do this with at least half of my layers.

Place a puff pastry layer on a serving plate. Spread 3 to 4 tablespoons of cream on it. Cover with a layer of puff pastry. Repeat the process with the remaining layers. Top the final layer with cream.

Decorate your cake with the excess pieces of puff pastry by crumbling them overtop your cake. Cover and refrigerate overnight.

Remove from the fridge 1 hour before serving. Store in the fridge, covered, for up to 5 days (although, let's be real, it's going to be gone within 24 hours).

NOTES:

I have tested making the cream with tapioca starch and arrowroot powder instead of cornstarch and have found the consistency to be a little runny for my taste. The flavor will still be there, but you will not get that perfectly-held-together cream you are looking for. Stick with cornstarch, if possible.

My favorite "incidentally vegan" puff pastry for this recipe is Tenderflake's.

7-Layer Saltines Squares

(CUSTOMIZABLE)

(NUT/SEED-FREE OPTION)

(EXTRA PREP)

MAKES: 16 SQUARES
PREPARATION: 15 MINUTES
COOKING: 30 MINUTES
RESTING: 1 HOUR

ONE DESSERT I MADE over a dozen times as a teenager is the classic 7 Layers Bars, also known as Magic Bars. This dessert always satisfied even my most intense sweet cravings. My new version is made with my very own Maple-Sweetened Condensed Milk (p. 273). It also features saltines, which, instead of being soaked in butter, are flavored with more of my homemade sweetened condensed milk. I chose saltines over graham crackers to keep these squares at a more moderate sweetness level. As you make this dessert, savor the process of layering the ingredients one on top of the other, from the decadent dairy-free chocolate chips, to the slightly bitter dark chocolate, roasted peanuts, and sweet raisins, to the rich shredded coconut. You can also have fun customizing this recipe with ingredients you love!

33 salted tops saltines, 1½ cups (110 g) when crushed

¾ cup (185 ml) Maple-Sweetened Condensed Milk (p. 273), divided

⅓ cup (55 g) dairy-free chocolate chips (see note)

⅓ cup (40 g) chopped dark chocolate (I use 70–85%) (see note)

½ cup (65 g) chopped salted roasted peanuts, optional (see note)

⅔ cup (100 g) sultana raisins (see note)

⅔ cup (65 g) unsweetened shredded coconut

Preheat the oven to 350°F. Line an 8-inch square baking dish with parchment paper, leaving overhang at both ends to serve as handles.

In a food processor, pulse the saltines until half are broken up into very small pieces and the other half remain as larger flakes. Transfer to a large mixing bowl.

Add ¼ cup and 2 tablespoons (90 ml) of the condensed milk. If your sweetened condensed milk has been in the fridge for a few hours, it will have thickened significantly. You will have to liquefy it before using by warming it in the microwave on high power for 30 seconds or in a small saucepan until it has a silky caramel texture.

Mix using a silicone spatula until the saltines are well coated and the mixture sticks together.

Transfer to the prepared baking dish and press down on the mixture with your spatula to create a uniform layer.

Top with the chocolate chips and dark chocolate. Layer with the peanuts, and then the raisins and shredded coconut.

CONTINUED ➤

Pour the remaining ¼ cup and 2 tablespoons (90 ml) of condensed milk overtop the coconut. I find that using a spoon to drizzle the condensed milk is the easiest way to distribute it somewhat evenly; it does not have to be spread perfectly evenly, though.

Bake for 30 minutes or until the coconut starts to brown.

For extra color, increase the heat to 500°F and broil for 1 to 2 minutes, until the coconut is more evenly golden brown; watch very closely so that it doesn't burn.

Remove the baking dish from the oven and place on a cooling rack. Let the slab cool in the baking dish for 30 minutes, then carefully lift it out of the dish, using the ends of the parchment as handles, and set on the cooling rack to cool for an additional 30 minutes before slicing into 16 squares.

Store at room temperature in an airtight container for up to 3 days.

NOTES:

I love to use a mixture of chocolate chips and dark chocolate, to balance out the sweetness in this dessert, but if you want these squares to be on the sweet side, use ⅔ cup (110 g) of chocolate chips and omit the dark chocolate; if you would like them to be less sweet, use ⅔ cup (80 g) of chopped dark chocolate and omit the chocolate chips.

If you have a nut allergy, omit the peanuts. Or if you just prefer using another nut, you absolutely can. Chopped pecans and walnuts work great.

If you don't have raisins, swap them out for dried cranberries.

I chose saltines to keep the sweetness level moderate, but if you want a sweeter dessert or if you do not have saltines on hand, feel free to swap them out with 1½ cups (150 g) of crushed cookies of choice. If you are using harder cookies like vegan graham cookies, make sure that no large chunks remain when processing.

Classic Chocolate Cake

(NUT/SEED-FREE) (EXTRA PREP)

MAKES: ONE 9-INCH CAKE
PREPARATION: 15 MINUTES
COOKING: 25 MINUTES
RESTING: 1 HOUR

MY PASSION for chocolate cake started when I was about twelve years old. What has always fascinated me is the sheer number of variations—from chocolate beet cakes, to no-flour chocolate cake, to gluten-free or keto versions, and so many more. To create this version, I dedicated time to many trials, as I had a specific goal in mind: a cake that was not overly sweet, made with a mixture of whole-wheat and all-purpose flour, sweetened with maple syrup, and featuring my favorite frosting ever: The Best Chocolate Frosting (p. 272). After testing and sharing dozens of cakes with family, this recipe was born. It is chocolatey, rich, and perfectly moist.

○ ○

1 cup (140 g) whole-wheat flour

1 cup (140 g) all-purpose flour

½ cup (50 g) Dutch-processed cocoa powder

1½ tsp baking powder

½ tsp baking soda

¼ tsp sea salt

¾ cup (185 ml) boiling water

1 tsp instant coffee powder

½ cup (125 ml) unsweetened soy milk

½ cup (125 ml) maple syrup

⅓ cup (80 ml) unsweetened applesauce

⅓ cup (80 ml) canola oil

2 tsp vanilla extract

1 tbsp (15 ml) balsamic vinegar

1 serving of The Best Chocolate Frosting (p. 272), chilled for at least 3 hours

GARNISHES, OPTIONAL
Chocolate shavings
Fresh raspberries

○ ○ ○

Preheat the oven to 350°F. Grease a 9-inch springform or regular cake pan with cooking spray or a neutral cooking oil (such as avocado, canola, or melted refined coconut).

In a mixing bowl, whisk together the whole-wheat flour, all-purpose flour, cocoa powder, baking powder, baking soda, and salt.

In a large mixing bowl, pour in the boiling water and sprinkle in the coffee powder. Stir to incorporate.

Whisk in the soy milk, maple syrup, applesauce, canola oil, vanilla extract, and balsamic vinegar.

Add the dry ingredients to the wet ingredients and whisk until combined and no streaks of flour remain—but be careful not to overmix.

Pour the batter into the prepared pan, smooth the top, and bake for 25 minutes or until a toothpick inserted into the center comes out clean.

Remove the cake from the oven and let cool for 5 minutes before removing from the pan and letting cool completely on a cooling rack.

Top with the frosting, and garnish with chocolate shavings and fresh raspberries, if desired. Store in the fridge in an airtight container for up to 3 days.

NOTE:

If you are serving a crowd, I recommend doubling the batter recipe and the frosting (p. 272) for an epic two-tiered, ultra-fudgy and chocolatey cake. Or, you could spread one serving of frosting between the layers and top the cake with coconut whipped cream and berries. This one, too, is a favorite!

Cranberry and Orange Muffins

(NUT/SEED-FREE)

MAKES: 10–12 MUFFINS
PREPARATION: 10 MINUTES
COOKING: 25 MINUTES

○

LIKE FOR MANY KIDS, one of my favorite outings growing up was going to McDonald's. Although I loved its savory menu, my mom and I always had a soft spot for the muffin and tea combos. We would both order a mint tea with cranberry and orange muffins, and enjoy them while my younger brothers ran around in the PlayPlace. This was our special time around a simple dessert and a cup of tea, to slow down and enjoy each other's company. Because those McDonald's muffins marked my childhood, I wanted to honor them in this book with my own plant-based version, featuring fresh fruits. As you make them, enjoy squeezing fresh juice out of your orange, zesting the peel (and smelling its citrusy aroma!), and folding the tangy cranberries into the batter. Pair these muffins with a cup of your favorite warm beverage (I opt for mint tea, to take me back to my teen years).

○ ○

2 cups (280 g) all-purpose flour, plus more for coating

2 tsp baking powder

¼ tsp baking soda

¼ tsp sea salt

½ cup (125 ml) freshly squeezed orange juice (see note)

½ cup (125 ml) soy milk

¼ cup (60 ml) canola oil

½ cup (100 g) organic cane sugar

Zest of 1 large orange

1 cup (3½ oz/100 g) fresh or frozen cranberries

○ ○ ○

Preheat the oven to 350°F. Grease a muffin pan with cooking spray or canola oil. Alternatively, you can line each muffin cup with a muffin liner.

In a large mixing bowl, whisk together the flour, baking powder, baking soda, and salt.

In a separate large mixing bowl, whisk together the orange juice, soy milk, canola oil, sugar, and orange zest.

Pour the dry mixture into the wet mixture and whisk until smooth and no flour streaks remain—but be careful not to overmix the batter. Set aside.

Sprinkle about 1 tablespoon of flour into an empty bowl. Add the cranberries and toss to coat.

Add the cranberries to the muffin batter, leaving behind the excess flour in the bowl. Fold in the cranberries using a silicone spatula.

Divide the batter among the muffin cups. If you want tall muffins, fill 10 muffin cups rather than 12.

Bake for 20 to 22 minutes, until a toothpick inserted into the center comes out clean.

Remove from the oven and let cool in the pan for 5 minutes, then transfer to a cooling rack to let cool completely. Store in the fridge in an airtight container for up to 3 days.

NOTE:

*I recommend zesting your orange using a Microplane grater
before juicing it.*

I view the recipes in this chapter as potential building blocks that can help round out various meals in this cookbook (and any of your own creations), while adding new layers of depth and flavor. The sauces, creams, and toppings featured generally require few ingredients, but I encourage you to continue applying this cookbook's philosophy in their preparation: tasting along the way, noticing the flavors bloom, and getting creative with their use in other dishes. They may be simple, but they are never lacking flavor or soul.

Scrumptious Sauces, Creams, and Toppings

Homemade Mayo

(CUSTOMIZABLE) (GLUTEN-FREE)
(NUT/SEED-FREE)

MAKES: 1½ CUPS
PREPARATION: 5 MINUTES

○ FLIPPING THROUGH THIS BOOK, you might have noticed that I love mayo. It is one of those beloved simple ingredients that can become, with a bit of prep and love, a wonderful addition to so many meals. It appears in a number of my recipes, including my Ultimate Breakfast Sandwich (p. 57), Shuba (p. 85), and Olivier Salad (p. 93). Although vegan mayo has become quite accessible for me in Canada over the past couple of years, I understand that it might not be for everyone, or it might be expensive where you live. So I want to share a homemade mayo recipe that is super easy to make, uses accessible ingredients, and costs up to five times less than store-bought mayo, especially if you choose to sub in a more affordable oil like canola oil.

○ ○

½ cup unsweetened soy milk (see note)

1 tsp lemon juice

1 tsp apple cider vinegar

1 tsp maple syrup

¼ tsp mustard powder

¼ tsp salt, plus more to taste

1 cup avocado oil (see note)

○ ○ ○

Blend all the ingredients except the oil in a high-speed blender on high speed for 10 seconds. Reduce the speed to medium-low, remove the lid or its center cap, and slowly pour in the oil with the motor running.

Replace the center cap or lid and increase the speed to high, blending for another 10 seconds or until thick and creamy, like traditional mayo. Taste and add more salt to your liking.

Store in the fridge in a lidded jar for up to 10 days.

NOTES:

Soy milk is the only milk that yields successful results every time for me, so I would not suggest substituting it with a different plant-based milk.

You can swap the avocado oil, if you prefer. Canola oil is an inexpensive alternative if you want your mayo to have a quite neutral taste. Grapeseed oil also works if you love its flavor, which has a subtly bitter quality to it. If you use olive oil, opt for one that is mild in flavor. But do not use coconut oil, as it will solidify when stored in the fridge.

If you do not have a high-speed blender, use an immersion blender. Simply put all the ingredients except the oil into the tall blender cup, blend for a few seconds, then slowly stream the oil into the mixture and blend until thick, moving the blender up and down.

Want to jazz up your mayo? After blending, fold in chopped fresh herbs such as dill, chives, parsley, basil, or oregano—or, for an extra kick, 1 to 3 tablespoons of smooth Dijon mustard. Or transform this mayo into my delicious and bright Tangy Aioli (p. 259).

Tangy Aioli

(GLUTEN-FREE) (NUT/SEED-FREE)
(EXTRA PREP)

MAKES: ½ CUP
PREPARATION: 5 MINUTES

THIS AIOLI IS TRULY what I think of when
thinking of a luxurious dipping sauce. Bright,
lemony, tangy, garlicky, and creamy, it is a perfect
condiment for anything from fries to roasted
veggies, like my Garlicky Roasted Potatoes (p. 106).
Paired with my Deep-Fried Oyster Mushrooms
(p. 123), the combo is the ultimate treat on a hot
summer day, along with a cold drink. It is also great
as a spread in sandwiches and wraps.

½ cup Homemade Mayo (p. 258)
  or store-bought vegan
  mayonnaise

3–4 garlic cloves, grated using a
  Microplane

1 tsp lemon zest

2 tbsp lemon juice, plus more
  to taste

Sea salt, to taste

Mix all the ingredients together in a small bowl, starting with
3 garlic cloves.

Taste and add more garlic, lemon juice, or salt to your liking.

Store in the fridge in an airtight container for up to 1 week.

Smoky Adobo Crema

(GLUTEN-FREE) (NUT/SEED-FREE)

MAKES: ½ CUP
PREPARATION: 5 MINUTES

IF YOU HAVE spent some time in the kitchen, you have probably experimented with creamy sauces made from mayo, butter, cream, or even blended cauliflower (yes, you can make alfredo sauce with cauliflower!). Silken tofu is another ingredient I love to use for my creamy cold sauces. It's velvety, blends up beautifully, and is a blank canvas for flavor. In this sauce, all the flavors build on each other: the chipotle peppers bring smokiness and heat, while the maple syrup adds sweetness, and the lemon juice a little tang. This slightly spicy and creamy sauce is delicious drizzled on top of Black Beans and Plantain Tacos (p. 181), spread on burgers, or even as a dipping sauce for roasted potato wedges.

5 oz (150 g) silken tofu, drained

1 tbsp chopped chipotle pepper in adobo sauce

1 tbsp maple syrup

1 tsp lemon juice

¼ tsp sea salt, plus more to taste

Blend the tofu, chipotle pepper, maple syrup, lemon juice, and salt in a mini food processor.

Transfer the adobo crema to a serving bowl and enjoy as a condiment.

Store in the fridge in an airtight container for up to 1 week.

NOTE:

If you don't have a mini food processor, you can use an immersion blender or a small blender like a nutribullet.

Tamari, Balsamic Vinegar, and Nutritional Yeast Sauce

(GLUTEN-FREE) (NUT/SEED-FREE)

MAKES: ½ CUP

PREPARATION: 5 MINUTES

THE FIRST TIME I made this sauce, I was not really thinking about turning it into a recipe. I didn't properly measure any of the ingredients, but just incorporated savory, umami flavors I was craving. Along the way, I kept tasting how the sauce was changing with the addition of each ingredient. I knew I had achieved exactly what I was looking for when I tasted this magical brown sauce and my eyes widened! How had I never put these ingredients together before? This sauce is really life-changing: It is creamy and salty. It has hints of umami and a cheesy aftertaste. It pairs wonderfully with roasted veggies (my Roasted Cauliflower on page 109 absolutely shines with this sauce too!) and makes for an amazing dressing for my Massaged Kale Salad (p. 97).

2 tbsp extra virgin olive oil

2 tbsp nutritional yeast

2 tbsp tamari

1 tbsp balsamic vinegar

2 tbsp runny tahini (see note)

1 tbsp water

1 tsp maple syrup

½ tsp whole grain Dijon mustard

¼ tsp garlic powder

Place all the ingredients in a small jar. Mix using a fork, then dress your favorite salad or roasted veggies.

Store in the fridge in an airtight container for up to 10 days.

NOTE:

If you don't have tahini on hand or have an allergy/intolerance to sesame seeds, replace it with natural roasted almond butter or cashew butter.

Nut-Free
Ricotta

GLUTEN-FREE   NUT/SEED-FREE

EXTRA PREP

MAKES: 1 CUP
PREPARATION: 10 MINUTES
COOKING: 30 MINUTES
RESTING: 1 HOUR 50 MINUTES

○ ○

4 cups unsweetened soy milk
  (see note)

1 tbsp + 1½ tsp white vinegar

⅛ tsp sea salt

NOTES:

*Do not use any other plant-based milk,
as the protein content in soy milk is
what allows it to separate.*

*It is important that you use nonreactive
materials when making this recipe. Opt
for a stainless steel, ceramic, or glass
saucepan as opposed to an aluminum,
cast-iron, or copper one. Also, use
wooden or silicone utensils when
handling the ricotta before cooling.*

○

I USED TO LOVE experimenting with ricotta in
both desserts and savory dishes. When it became
inaccessible to me after going vegan, I went on a quest
to discover how dairy ricotta is made—this discovery
was my saving grace! Just like with dairy ricotta,
boiling soy milk to exactly 185°F and then adding in
an acidic element causes the soy milk's protein and
fat to separate from the liquid. This recipe requires
extra love and attention, especially during the boiling
process. Try not to multitask! Be fully aware when
the milk is heating, to ensure you end up with the
right texture of ricotta. Once the mixture is drained,
you are left with a rich, creamy, spreadable ricotta
that works in a wide array of recipes, including my
Herby Mushroom and Ricotta Toasts (p. 50), Stewed
Blackberries and Lemon Ricotta Toasts (p. 49), and
Ricotta and Spinach Phyllo Cups (p. 111).

○ ○ ○

In a saucepan (see note), heat the soy milk over medium heat,
uncovered, until it reaches 185°F on a kitchen thermometer, stirring
often with a wooden spoon or silicone spatula.

Immediately stir in the vinegar and salt (don't worry if this causes a
variation in temperatures by a few degrees either way). Cook for an
additional 2 minutes, stirring often to prevent the mixture from boiling
over. The mixture will curdle—this is completely normal. Remove from
the heat, cover, and let sit for 20 minutes.

In the meantime, place a sieve over a large bowl. Line the sieve with
2 to 4 layers of cheesecloth (depending on how tightly knit your
cheesecloth is—the tighter the knit, the fewer layers you will need).
Make sure the entire surface of the sieve is covered.

Slowly pour the mixture into the lined sieve. I like to do this in two
to three batches to allow the liquid time to drain between pours. You
can also help the draining process by using a silicone spatula to stir
the mixture around in the sieve.

Let the mixture sit for 30 minutes to 1 hour 30 minutes, until the
ricotta reaches your desired consistency. (When I use two layers of
tightknit cheesecloth, I find that the perfect texture is achieved at
about the 30-minute mark.) Store in the fridge in an airtight container
for up to 1 week.

Maple Butter

(GLUTEN-FREE) (NUT/SEED-FREE)

MAKES: 2 CUPS
PREPARATION: 30 MINUTES
COOKING: 30 MINUTES
RESTING: 15 MINUTES

MAPLE BUTTER, also known as maple cream, is one of those heavenly spreads that deserves more recognition than it gets. First off, it is not available everywhere in the world, but also, even here in Canada, maple butter is only easy to find in late winter and early spring. But you can actually make this divine spread yourself, any day of the year! It is simple to make, but it does require patience, presence, focus, and a thermometer. As the maple syrup rises in temperature, it will start to boil up, so be fully present to prevent any spillover. Furthermore, to transform the maple syrup into a luxurious cream, you will have to use your stirring skills to aerate it, turning it into a thick mixture. The result will be a creamy, rich, and sweet maple spread so delicious you'd be forgiven for thinking it came straight out of a Quebec sugar shack!

1 (18 oz/540 ml) can grade A dark maple syrup

Pour the maple syrup into a tall, medium saucepan (with enough space for the maple syrup to boil up about 5 inches) and heat over medium heat, without stirring. Watch closely to make sure the maple syrup does not overflow. Once the maple syrup reaches 220°F, place ice cubes in a large metal bowl—enough to cover the bottom—and place a smaller saucepan or metal bowl on top of the ice. (The maple syrup is continuing to heat while you do this.)

Once the maple syrup reaches 235°F, after about 25 to 30 minutes in total, pour it into the small saucepan. Let the mixture cool to 99°F, about 15 minutes.

Remove the saucepan from the bowl of ice and place on a kitchen towel on the counter.

Using a wooden spoon (opt for one you do not use for savory dishes), stir the mixture constantly for 20 to 30 minutes. The syrup's maple color will turn to a more salted caramel color and finally it will become light beige, similar in color to creamed honey or tahini. Once the mixture is thick and creamy and gives you resistance when stirring, leaving circular strokes as you stir, the maple butter is ready.

Transfer immediately to a glass jar and store in the fridge, sealed, for up to 3 weeks. Enjoy on buttered toast or in my Maple Apple Galette (p. 239).

Bright Chopped Salsa

(GLUTEN-FREE) (NUT/SEED-FREE)

MAKES: 1½ CUPS
PREPARATION: 10 MINUTES
RESTING: 30 MINUTES

○

FOR THE LONGEST TIME, I couldn't understand the hype around salsa (yes, I know!). I think this was because all the salsa I had tried was store-bought, not homemade. Let me tell you, the first time I made my own, I got it. I am in the "chunky salsa" camp, so I chop all my ingredients by hand to achieve my perfect texture—if you love the smoother kind, use a food processor to break down the tomato to your desired consistency. My key to leveling up my salsa's flavor: grating the garlic using a Microplane. This really brings out the garlicky flavor and adds a delightful kick. You can also let your chopped tomatoes release some of their water by letting them sit in a sieve with a little bit of salt for 30 minutes, which helps concentrate the tomato flavor. This salsa goes well with chips, tacos, burgers, and especially my Crispy Chickpea Pancakes (p. 41).

○ ○

1 large tomato (I like beefsteak), cut in ¼-inch pieces

¾ tsp sea salt, divided

¼ cup finely diced red onion

¼ packed cup chopped fresh coriander

1 tbsp lime juice

¼ tsp black pepper

Pinch of cayenne pepper, optional

1 garlic clove

○ ○ ○

In a sieve placed over a bowl, stir the tomatoes and ½ teaspoon of salt to distribute the salt evenly. (If you prefer a smooth salsa, first blend the tomatoes in a food processor to your desired consistency, then transfer to the sieve with the salt.)

Let sit for 15 minutes to release some of the water from the tomatoes, then stir directly in the sieve and taste. If you prefer a stronger flavor, let the tomatoes sit for another 15 minutes, to drain more water. Use a silicone spatula to gently press down on the tomato pieces to extract more tomato water.

Transfer the mixture to a bowl along with the remaining ¼ teaspoon of salt, red onion, coriander, lime juice, pepper, and cayenne, if using.

Use a Microplane to grate the garlic into the salsa. Alternatively, you can very finely mince it. Stir.

Taste and adjust seasonings by adding more salt, lime juice for acidity, or cayenne for heat, if desired. Store in the fridge in an airtight container for up to 24 hours.

Pickled Onions

(CUSTOMIZABLE) (GLUTEN-FREE)
(NUT/SEED-FREE) (EXTRA PREP)

MAKES: 2 CUPS
PREPARATION: 5 MINUTES
COOKING: 5 MINUTES
RESTING: 2 HOURS

○

I LOVE THE BALANCE acidity can bring to dishes, whether it comes from a spritz of citrus or a drizzle of vinegar. Garnishing any dish with a pickled vegetable is an easy way to add an extra kick. What's great about this pickled onions recipe is how customizable it is. You can add some heat to your onions by pickling them with sliced jalapeños or habaneros, and/or add freshness by pickling them with herbs such as dill or rosemary. The options are endless! In terms of time, the longer they pickle, the better they get. After an hour, taste your pickled onions and notice their light pickling. You can repeat this process after another hour, then again a full day later (my preferred total pickling time) and taste how much more robust the flavors have become. Enjoy these pickled onions on your tacos, in burgers, on your tofu scrambles, in salads, or in my Ultimate Breakfast Sandwich (p. 57).

○ ○

1 red onion, thinly sliced

2 garlic cloves, coarsely chopped

2 tsp whole peppercorns

½ tsp cumin seeds

½ tsp nigella seeds (see note)

1 cup white vinegar (see note)

2 tsp granulated sugar

½ tsp sea salt

○ ○ ○

In a 16-oz mason jar, place the onion, garlic, peppercorns, cumin seeds, and nigella seeds.

In a small saucepan, heat the white vinegar, sugar, and salt over medium heat until the sugar and salt have dissolved, stirring occasionally using a silicone spatula—no need to bring this mixture to a boil.

Pour into the mason jar and seal with the lid. Shake the jar to distribute the garlic pieces, peppercorns, cumin seeds, and nigella seeds somewhat evenly. Set the jar upright, remove the lid, and poke the floating onions down until they're fully submerged.

Put the lid back on and place in the fridge to pickle for at least 2 hours and up to 24 hours.

Store in the fridge in an airtight container for up to 3 weeks.

NOTES:

If you don't have nigella seeds, use 1 teaspoon of black cumin or more regular cumin seeds.

If you don't have white vinegar, swap it with apple cider vinegar or red wine vinegar.

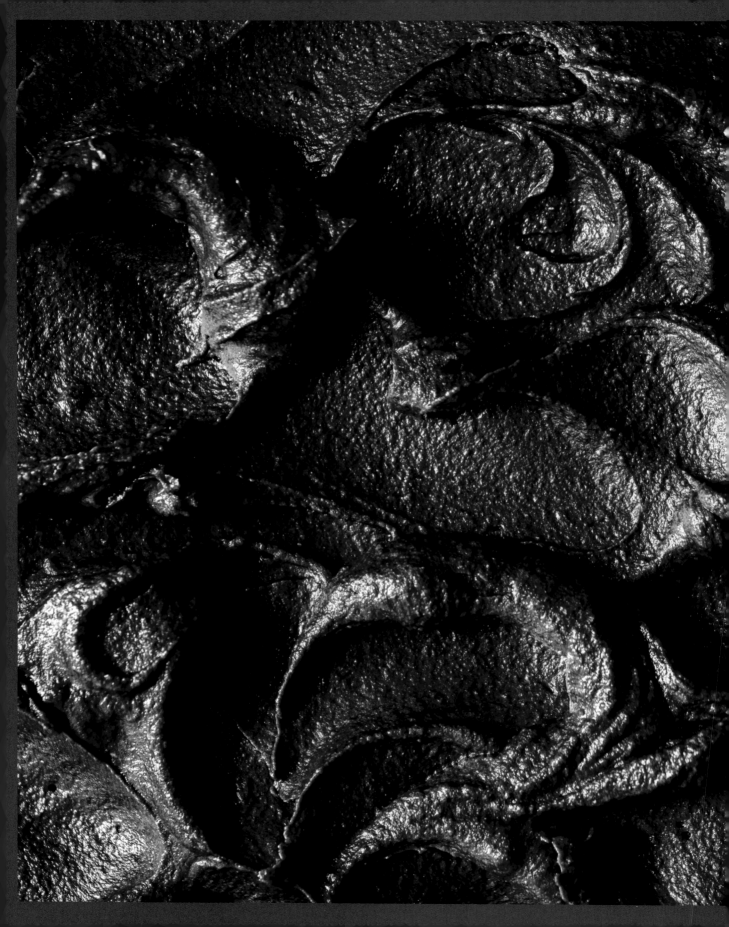

Date-Sweetened Leek and Onion Jam

(GLUTEN-FREE) (NUT/SEED-FREE)

MAKES: 1½ CUPS
PREPARATION: 5 MINUTES
COOKING: 35 MINUTES

○

WHEN I BEGAN to develop my own cooking style, I often gravitated toward sweet and salty flavor combinations. It was only on Christmas Day a few years ago that I got the idea of creating a sweet and salty onion jam (inspired by an epic tomato jam I had had in Spain), as a pairing for vegan cheeses. Little did I know that I had created a recipe that works well not only with crackers and cheese but also as an amazing topping for my mac and cheese, tacos, and burgers. It can even be served as part of a holiday plate alongside mashed potatoes, vegan turkey, and cranberry sauce. Be mindful to keep the heat low when making this jam: too high and it crisps up the onions and leeks. A low heat allows the alliums to soften and caramelize, resulting in a luxurious spread.

○ ○

1 tsp avocado oil

1 large red onion, cut in half lengthwise and sliced (see note)

2 leeks (light green and white parts only), cut in half lengthwise and then into half-moons

2 garlic cloves, minced

⅓ cup packed pitted soft dates (such as Bam or Medjool), coarsely chopped

1 tbsp balsamic vinegar

1 tsp rice vinegar

½ tsp black pepper

¼ tsp sea salt, plus more to taste

○ ○ ○

Heat the avocado oil in a large pan set over medium heat. Add the red onion and leeks. Cook for 12 to 15 minutes, until the onion and leeks are softened, stirring occasionally with a wooden spoon.

Add the garlic and dates. Using your wooden spoon, try to break apart the dates a little and stir.

Reduce the heat to low, cover, and cook, stirring occasionally, for 20 minutes or until the onion has caramelized and the mixture has reduced by more than half.

Turn off the heat and stir in the balsamic vinegar, rice vinegar, pepper, and salt.

Let the mixture cool before transferring to an airtight container. Store in the fridge for up to 2 weeks.

NOTES:

If you don't have red onion, swap it out with yellow onion.

Enjoy this jam chilled or brought to room temperature on toasts with vegan cheese, in my Burger for the Non-vegans (p. 143), sandwiches, or even as a topping on Smoky Sweet Potato Mac and Cheese (p. 135).

Date-Sweetened Chia Jam

(CUSTOMIZABLE)   (GLUTEN-FREE)
(NUT/SEED-FREE)

MAKES: 1 CUP
PREPARATION: 10 MINUTES
COOKING: 15 MINUTES
RESTING: 45 MINUTES

CHIA JAMS ARE a staple in the vegan community, and because I love to give my own spin on classic dishes, I want to share the version my mom and I have been making for a few years, one that is sweetened entirely by fruit and is incredibly versatile. You can use any kind of frozen berries, and even experiment using a few of your favorite types together. Have fun with it (and use up any straggling berries in your freezer—you know, those berries you hand-picked in the spring and froze). My favorite version is made with a mix of raspberries, strawberries, and cranberries. This jam is delightfully sweet, has a lovely hint of acidity, spreads really well, and keeps for a while, which makes it a great staple to have in your fridge!

2 cups frozen berries of choice
   (see note)

⅓ cup packed pitted soft dates
   (such as Bam or Medjool)

2 tbsp lemon juice

2 tbsp whole chia seeds

In a saucepan, bring the frozen berries, dates, and lemon juice to a boil over high heat, uncovered, stirring often with a silicone spatula. I like to press down on the dates during this process to help them soften faster.

Once the mixture is boiling and the berries have thawed, reduce the heat to low and simmer, covered, for 10 minutes. Remove from the heat and let cool, uncovered, for 15 minutes.

Transfer to an immersion blender or a small blender and blend the mixture until smooth, or to your desired consistency.

Transfer the mixture to a wide-mouth mason jar and let cool for 30 minutes, then stir in the chia seeds.

Store in the fridge in an airtight jar for up to 2 weeks. Enjoy on toast or with oatmeal, yogurt, or in my Strawberry Swirl Breakfast Muffins (p. 32).

NOTE:

The berry possibilities are endless, from raspberries, strawberries, or cherries to blueberries, blackberries, cranberries, even blackcurrants. If you're using a combination, just make sure you have 2 cups of berries in total.

The Best Chocolate Frosting

(CUSTOMIZABLE) (GLUTEN-FREE)
(NUT/SEED-FREE) (EXTRA PREP)

MAKES: 1 CUP
PREPARATION: 15 MINUTES
RESTING: 3 HOURS

WHEN I THINK of adding a little luxury to my life through food, I think of chocolate and I think of this frosting. Three ingredients, no butter, no powdered sugar—and yet, this frosting is absolutely divine! It's thick but spreadable, just like a butter-based frosting. Its sweetness comes from the dates and the dark chocolate's sugar. The richness and creaminess come from the coconut milk and the cocoa butter in the chocolate. Because the dates add so much sweetness, opt for a dark chocolate—70% or higher is ideal (any lower and it could be overly sweet). This frosting is delicious on virtually any baked good, but my favorite (and extra luxurious!) ways to enjoy it are on my Classic Chocolate Cake (p. 253) or Grand Marnier Crepe Cake (p. 221).

½ cup packed pitted dates of choice (any kind works; I prefer Bam, Medjool, or Noor)

Boiling water

½ cup full-fat coconut milk

½ cup chopped dark chocolate (I use 85%)

Pinch of sea salt

Place the dates in a bowl and cover with boiling water. Cover the bowl with a plate, and let sit for 10 minutes.

Heat the coconut milk in the microwave on high power for 30 seconds to 1 minute, or on the stovetop in a saucepan over medium heat, until warm to the touch; don't let it boil.

Drain the dates (save the water; it's a delicious sweetener for smoothies and oatmeal) and transfer to a high-speed blender or a food processor. Add the warm coconut milk, dark chocolate, and salt. Blend until totally smooth, scraping down the sides of the blender as needed to make sure all the bits and pieces are well blended.

Transfer to an airtight container and chill for 3 hours or until thickened enough to be spreadable while also holding its shape when frosting a cake.

Remove from the fridge and frost your favorite treats. Store in the fridge in an airtight container for up to 5 days.

NOTES:

This recipe makes enough to frost a single-layer cake. If using for my Grand Marnier Crepe Cake (p. 221), double the recipe and add the zest of 1 orange and 4 teaspoons of Grand Marnier before blending.

If the frosting has set too much, warm it up at room temperature for 15 to 30 minutes before using.

Maple-Sweetened Condensed Milk

GLUTEN-FREE   NUT/SEED-FREE

EXTRA PREP

MAKES: 1 CUP
PREPARATION: 5 MINUTES
COOKING: 1 HOUR 10 MINUTES
RESTING: 8 HOURS 15 MINUTES

I HAVE TRIED a good number of store-bought sweetened condensed nondairy substitutes and have frequently been disappointed—mostly because the mixture always seemed to separate and be way too thick for my liking. By making your own sweetened condensed milk, not only do you save money, but there is something so satisfying about being actively involved in making your own perfectly smooth and creamy sweetened condensed milk. I love making this recipe to sweeten my iced coffee (it brings to mind Vietnamese coffee) and using it in my childhood classic, 7-Layer Saltines Squares (p. 249).

1 (13½ oz/400 ml) can full-fat coconut milk

⅔ cup maple syrup

In a saucepan, combine the coconut milk and maple syrup. Stirring occasionally, bring the mixture to a boil over medium-high heat, 8 to 10 minutes.

Reduce the heat to medium-low and continue cooking, uncovered, for 1 hour or until the mixture has thickened and darkened in color, coats the back of a spoon, and has reduced by about half. Stir every 5 minutes or so using a whisk, without scraping the sides of the saucepan, as you will notice that a crystalized rim will form overtime and you want to keep your condensed milk smooth.

Pour into a glass jar and let cool, uncovered, for 15 minutes before placing in the fridge, covered, for at least 8 hours to cool completely. Store in the fridge for up to 10 days.

NOTE:

Once your sweetened condensed milk has been in the fridge for a few hours, it will thicken considerably. You can liquefy it by warming it up in the microwave on medium power for 30 seconds, or in a small saucepan set over medium-low heat until it has a silky caramel texture.

Acknowledgments

If someone had told the 12-year-old Murielle who experimented in her parents' kitchen every weekend that one day she would be creating a book full of her memories, many of her family recipes, and hundreds of images she shot, she would never have believed it. And yet, here I am today, having poured so much of my heart and creativity into this project. This entire adventure has been one of the most challenging, yet rewarding experiences of my life. I am grateful to every single individual who, through their knowledge, love, and support, helped bring this book to life.

To my mom, Olga, who has always been one of my biggest supporters, thank you for believing in me. For reminding me to take it one day at a time whenever things get hard, including many times while working on this big project. Your strength, courage, and devotion to our family has been one of the biggest gifts I was given.

To Sam, my love—who knows whether I would be doing this if not for you? You encouraged me to pick up my first DSLR camera in 2012 and have always supported me in my creative ventures. You were the first person to ever ask me if one day I would want to write a cookbook because you saw it was something I was capable of, way before I ever saw it in myself. Thank you for the dozens of cookbooks you gave me through the years, always telling me that one day you'd walk into a bookstore and see my book on the shelves. Thank you for being my tester-in-chief, for giving me hugs whenever working on this manuscript felt like a mountain I could not climb up, for helping me rephrase sentences whenever I doubted my writing abilities, for squeezing a laugh out of me every time you told me *this* recipe was "your favorite one." Your love and support means more than you can imagine.

To my brothers, Luc and Samuel, thank you for your unwavering love and support and for often reminding me that I can always count on you.

To my dad, Cyrille, thank you for reminding me to stay connected to my roots and honor my history.

To my in-laws, the McKinnon clan, thank you for always encouraging me to embrace my creativity, pursue new ventures, and share my gifts with the world.

To my childhood friend, Anca, thank you for taking me out to celebrate right when I learned I was going to work on this cookbook and for never doubting that a project this big would be within reach.

To Elizabeth Emery, Diala Canelo, Livhuwani Tshikhudo, and Sadia Badiei, your friendship has been a source of joy, comfort, and peace through the years. Thank you for listening to me whenever I shared any of the difficulties I encountered throughout the process of writing this book.

To Aisha, your confidence in my work and in my ability to bring this project to completion was a source of strength. Thank you for your positivity and for the input you gave me throughout this process.

To Becca, our email exchanges over the years were always a dose of encouragement and joy, thank you.

To the team at Carl Social Club, past and present, including Laurence, Estelle, Fanny, Queenie, Julien, Joannie, Edward, Chloé, and Charles-Edouard, thank you for helping me push my creative boundaries through the various projects you bring me on and for cheering me on at every step of the creation of this book.

Thank you to Laura Wright, Nisha Vora, Alexandra Daum, and Hannah Che for seeing all the heart and love that went into creating this cookbook and for believing that it has a place on many readers' bookshelves.

To Rob Firing, my agent, thank you for believing in my vision from the very first moment we chatted over Zoom.

Of course, thank you, from the bottom of my heart, to the team of people who were in the creative trenches with me as I brought this book to life.

Lindsay Paterson, your excitement about this cookbook and my vision gave me the confidence I needed to give myself fully to this project, knowing that I was supported. Whitney Millar, thank you for your devotion to this manuscript. All your comments, encouragements, and edits were always incredibly relevant. Judith Phillips, thank you for bearing with all my uses of "wonderful," "lovely," and "great" and for making this manuscript so clear and accessible to readers.

Jennifer Griffiths, I could not have asked for a more skilled designer to design my book. You created a design that beautifully reflects my aesthetic and makes my recipes and photos shine. Thank you.

Robert McCullough, thank you for welcoming me with open arms to the Appetite family and for being a supporter of this book from the first moment you heard about it.

Thank you to Michelle Arbus for noticing my work in the sea of photographers and recipe developers and for believing I had what it takes to write a cookbook.

To anyone at Appetite and Penguin Random House Canada who has helped from near or far to refine the vision for this book or helped bring it to life, thank you so much.

Thank you to all the people who have, through the years, supported my work in one way or another. To all the people who have messaged me on Instagram, commented on any one of my posts, or subscribed to my newsletter, you are one of the reasons I have continued creating through the years. You reminded me that my voice deserved to be heard, and I am forever grateful for that.

And finally, thank you to everyone who picked up this book and who has made (or plans to make) any of my recipes. I hope that you can feel the love I put into each recipe and that, as you spend time with each dish, you are able to savor the pleasure of cooking and share the love for it with those around you.

Index